MORE MONEY
than BRAINS

Also by Laura Penny:

Your Call Is Important to Us

MORE MONEY *than* BRAINS

WHY SCHOOL SUCKS, COLLEGE IS CRAP, & IDIOTS THINK THEY'RE RIGHT

LAURA PENNY

McClelland & Stewart

For my family and my fellow nerds

Library and Archives Canada Cataloguing in Publication

Penny, Laura, 1975-
More money than brains : why schools suck, college is crap, and idiots think they're right / Laura Penny.

ISBN 978-0-7710-7048-8

1. Canada – Intellectual life – 21st century. 2. United States – Intellectual life – 21st century. 3. Education – Aims and objectives – Canada. 4. Education – Aims and objectives – United States. 5. Educational sociology – Canada. 6. Educational sociology – United States. 7. Canada – Civilization – 21st century. 8. United States – Civilization – 21st century. I. Title.

LA192.P45 2010   306.097109'0511   C2009-905222-9

We acknowledge the financial support of the Government of Canada through the Book Publishing Industry Development Program and that of the Government of Ontario through the Ontario Media Development Corporation's Ontario Book Initiative. We further acknowledge the support of the Canada Council for the Arts and the Ontario Arts Council for our publishing program.

Published simultaneously in the United States by McClelland & Stewart Ltd., P.O. Box 1030, Plattsburgh, New York 12901
Library of Congress Control Number: 2010921954

ANCIENT FOREST
FRIENDLY

This book is printed on ancient-forest friendly paper.

Typeset in Minion by M&S, Toronto
Printed and bound in Canada

McClelland & Stewart Ltd.
75 Sherbourne Street
Toronto, Ontario
M5A 2P9
www.mcclelland.com

1 2 3 4 5   14 13 12 11 10

CONTENTS

A portrait of the author as a young Poindexter.

Chapter One

DON'T NEED NO EDJUMACATION

———

When I was a bespectacled baby nerd, pudgy, precocious prey for bullies, my parents consoled me with a beautiful lie. Someday, in magical places called college and work, being smart would be cool. I'd have the last laugh while the bullies were slaving away at crummy jobs. My mom and dad said youth was their time to shine, the high point for the popular, truculent lunkheads who mocked spelling bees and science fairs. Their lives would be all downhill after grade 12. Then nerds like me would become doctors and lawyers and maybe even prime minister, and profit from the dimwittedness of our former tormentors. Let 'em have their stupid dances and hockey games, they said. The future belonged to the weird kids who dug microscopes and dictionaries.

This, like many of my parents' reassuring fibs, was partly true. There was no Santa, but there were plenty of Santas in the malls every December. The power of nerdiness did indeed propel many of my fellow Poindexters into respectable professions. The Poindexters – the pallid, indoorsy, owlish sorts who always got picked last for teams – have become coders and chemists and brokers and communications experts. But the struggle between bullies and nerds certainly did not end, as promised, when we graduated. Nor do nerds always emerge victorious in the contests of adult life. The bullies persevered and proliferated, went online and on TV and the radio, into politics and industry, and found new venues for numerous variations on a familiar theme: *Fuck you, four-eyes.*

I am not surprised that bullies continue to hate nerds, that the dudes who shove weedy science fair winners into lockers grow up to reject carbon taxes and vote for "strong" leaders. No, what shocks me is the number of self-hating nerds who are willing to pander to the bullies, the countless pundits and politicos who deploy their A-student skills in the service of anti-intellectualism.

This anti-intellectualism is at odds with all our talk about the importance of good schools. North Americans lavish a lot of rhetoric and resources on education. Politicians, pundits, business leaders, and concerned citizens natter on about the need to train workers to stay competitive in a global information economy, where knowledge is power. Post-secondary enrolment has reached record highs and private colleges of varying legitness have sprung up all over North America to cater to our seemingly insatiable hunger for classes. We also spend millions on books, toys, DVDs, video games, and supplements that claim to boost young – or aging – brains.

Never have so many been so schooled! But all this extra education has not turned the majority of North Americans into nerds, or nerdophiles. Our well-intentioned attempts to push and prod every semi-sentient kid through university seem to be backfiring. More people spending money and time on degrees has produced a surprising toxic side effect: more people who hate school – and nerds.

The bachelor's degree has become a costly high-school diploma, the new middle-class normal. Ergo, higher ed has been demoted to the level of a racket, a swindle, a series of pointless exertions one must complete to get the golden ticket to a good job. Listen to talk radio, watch Fox News, and you'll learn that nerds are the real bullies. We dastardly bastards run the continent's most widespread and shameless kid-snatching operation, spiriting people's beloved offspring away for years so we can make them think (and drink) strange things for our own amusement and enrichment. The con has gone so well that we've started hustling suckers of all ages, luring hard-working adults and innocent seniors into our cunning scholastic traps. We extort money, effort, and time from taxpayers, students, and their families by threatening them with the dread spectre of unemployability. Then we teach material our students will never, ever use at work – or anywhere else, for that matter. What do we know-it-alls know about work? It's not like any of us has ever been there or done any.

Some of the people who spin this spiel are dropouts, such as Glenn Beck and Rush Limbaugh, who matriculated in morning-zoo shows and Top 40 Countdown radio. Beck and Limbaugh present their lack of academic credentials as proof of their moral and intellectual purity. At the same time, they ape the academics they claim to abhor: Limbaugh refers to himself as a professor from the Limbaugh Institute of Advanced Conservative Studies, and Beck scribbles Byzantine charts on a chalkboard as if he's lecturing undergrads.

Then there are all their fellow-travellers, folks like Ann Coulter and Mark Levin, who have perfectly respectable degrees from elite schools – the very academic institutions they incessantly deride. Politicians such as Dubya and Mitt Romney pull the same act. *Pay no attention to my fancy degree or Harvard M.B.A. or the family fortunes that funded my first-class credentials. I'm a commonsensical commoner, a straight-talkin' shitkicker just like you.*

This exceedingly cynical summary of education – that it is a swindle perpetrated by sophists – is not that much of an exaggeration, alas. I've seen this view of education, phrased in much more vulgar terms, on many a message board. I've encountered more genteel versions of it in political speeches, editorials, and letters to the editor. This dismissive attitude is also evident in other popular phrases. *Overeducated* is now common parlance. Yet you never hear that someone is over-rich or oversexy. *Perpetual student* is rarely a ringing endorsement of someone's commitment to "lifelong learning," to bum a bit of educratic euphemese. When we come across terms such as *academic* or *theoretical* in the media, they usually mean "irrelevant" or "imaginary," mere mental exercises at a remove from the serious business of life. "You think you're so smart" is never a compliment; the only thing worse than being smart is thinking that you are.

This attitude affects the way students approach university. Many want to get credentials that guarantee them super-awesome careers, but they don't need no edjumacation. I've taught useless liberal-artsy subjects such as English and philosophy for a decade, and some of my students have been quite frank. *No offence, Miss, but reading, thinking, and writing are wastes of time and boring as hell.* They were never gonna *use* English . . . even though they had to do precisely that to bitch about its uselessness.

I love teaching, but there are days when I feel like a god-damn cartwright, like a practitioner and proponent of archaic and eccentric arts the kids will not need in the glorious anal-phabetic future. Sonnets, semicolons, and history might as well be alchemy or phrenology. As long as, like, people can, like, understand you, like, what's the diff, y'know? Nobody cares about that old stuff. Nobody understands those long words. Nobody ever got hired because they could parse rhyme schemes or pick an argument apart or write a sentence, except for nerds like me, who squander our lives totally overanalyz-ing every little thing.

It would be a gross generalization to simply say that North Americans are ignorant and anti-intellectual. That would also make a really short book; I could print it in a hundred-point font, illustrate it with pictures of boobs and monster trucks, and then wait to see if it proved itself with boffo sales. It is more accurate to say that North Americans have a love-hate relationship with knowledge. We overestimate the value and reliability of certain uses of intelligence and can be quite dis-dainful towards mental pursuits that do not result in new stocks, synthetic foodstuffs, pills, or modes of conveyance. If we're going to endure the insufferable tedium of learning, we do so for one reason: to make the big bucks.

We have, for the past few decades, steadily favoured money over brains. This is not to say that the moneyed are stupid. No, sir! The money-minded would not be so very moneyed if they were not armed with intellect, if they had not invested gross-buckets in their own stable of brains. It takes a surfeit of intellect to create complex financial instruments such as derivatives or to convince people that they need to deodorize, adorn, or alter yet another part of their body. The difference between money and brains is not a matter of how much either side of this divide knows. No, the big difference is the way they see knowledge and why they think intelligence is good. When I say "money," I mean those who think you learn to earn, that our relation to knowledge is instrumental. When I say "brains," I mean those who want to learn, who see knowing as an end in itself rather than the means to an end.

The mental work we have been exhorted to pursue is valuable because it is lucrative, not because it is smart. The kinds of thinking we have praised and celebrated, like the innovations of the Internet geek and the heroic entrepreneur or the efficiency of the ruthless CEO, are shrewd, technical ways of assessing the world, interpretations that turn complex states of affairs into calculable measures such as commodity prices and page clicks.

The irony is that our overwhelming emphasis on money, our conviction that markets are the smartest systems of all, has resulted in three recessions and one global market meltdown in the past thirty years. The more-money-than-brains mindset has obvious disadvantages for brains, and the 2008 fiscal collapse suggests that it is not so great for money either. But this crash also gives North Americans a chance to reassess our values and reconsider what we want from our political institutions, education systems, and markets. It is an opportune moment to think about we think about thinking, to examine our domestic intelligence failures and recalibrate the relation between money and brains.

The most obvious example of this shift is Barack Obama's victory in the 2008 U.S. election, which pundits described as a victory for brains, a *Revenge of the Nerds* moment after the long, idiotic Bush nightmare. Carlin Romano, a professor and critic, wrote an article for the *Chronicle of Higher Education* in 2009 that sums up this sentiment nicely: "Philosopher-prez in chief and cosmopolitan in chief. After all this time, you figure, we were entitled to one. It looks as if we've got him."[1]

Obama has made admirable statements about education and his own good old-fashioned liberal arts degree. This is, admittedly, pretty sweet after nearly a decade of presidential pissing in the general direction of fancy book-learnin'. But I think it is way too hasty and optimistic to assume that Obama's election means smarts are cool again, and that America resolves henceforth to be kinder and gentler to its oft-mocked eggheads.

Saying that Obama's win marks the end of anti-intellectualism is a lot like saying it means the end of racism. Sure, it's a good sign, but it's not like the guy is six feet of anti-dote. Moreover, Obama's presidency has inspired a seething right-wing backlash and stupefying coverage of his every snooty foible and flash of hauteur. Jeez, President College can't even eat right like regular people! When he visited a greasy burger joint for the express purpose of supping with slovenly commoners, he had the audacity to request Dijon, a notoriously French mustard. A sign of Eurosocialist allegiances? *Bien sûr.*

The post-electoral Republican leadership vacuum was promptly filled by some of the right's most gleefully proficient nerd-bashers, figures such as Sarah Palin, Glenn Beck, and Rush Limbaugh. All present themselves as mavericks, the only ones brave enough to speak emotive truth to factual power, outsiders marginalized by the uppity chattering classes in Hollywood, New York, and Washington.

These pseudo-populists insist that intellectuals are the real idiots. Ivy League city types think they are so smart, but that only goes to show how deluded and distant from common sense they are. As St. Ronald Reagan said in one of his most famous speeches – 1964's "A Time for Choosing" – "it's not that our liberal friends are ignorant. It's just that they know so much that isn't so." The right-wing message is loud and clear: complex matters like climate change and foreign relations and the economy are complex because the elitists and the bureaucrats make them that way, to serve their own agendas and exclude just plain folks from the political process. Have any of these brainiacs ever done something *really* complicated, like run a Podunk town or make payroll? Didn't think so!

The most rudimentary business skills or beavering one's

way to bosshood beat teaching or studying at some of the world's finest universities. Once we've established that universities are a joke, a fiendishly elaborate scheme to overcharge people for beer, it is easy to discount any body of facts or ostensible expertise that emanates from them. If expertise in general is fake, a self-serving liberal chimera, then it stands to reason that experts are the biggest frauds of all: empty suits who have nothing to offer but words and dipsy-doodle ideas they expect working people to pay for. The people and the pols become fact-proof, and those who huck information at them align themselves with the patronizing pedants of Team Pantywaist.

This sort of anti-intellectualism is not new. It has been part of American political life ever since Andrew Jackson played the role of Old Hickory. Canadians like to fancy themselves above this sort of pseudo-populist politicking and think that it is the neighbours' problem. But the Conservative Party's campaigns against Liberal leaders Stéphane Dion and Michael Ignatieff were just as anti-intellectual, in their own stolid Canadian way, as the invective of the red-meat, red-state crowds at McCain-Palin rallies or anti-tax tea parties.

Professors like Romano, and the mainstream press, have covered Obama's cosmopolitanism approvingly. They hope it will help ameliorate American relations with the rest of the world. Of course, this is also one of the things that drives Obama's detractors wild. Drawing huge crowds in Europe, pronouncing Middle Eastern place names correctly, and nabbing a Nobel for nothing are all suspect. Being far'n-friendly is an un-American affectation.

Stephen Harper and company appealed to the Canadian version of this provincial small-mindedness when they ran negative ads that sneered at Ignatieff for describing himself as "horribly cosmopolitan." His success in and familiarity with foreign lands was not an asset. No, instead he was cheating on Canada, whoring around with the likes of the BBC and Harvard.

I am not a fan of the man, but the Con campaign against him is so frigging brutal it makes me want to like Count Iggy. Consider this gem from their website, Ignatieff.me:

> . . . Ignatieff has written next-to-nothing about the economy – the most pressing issue facing Canada (and the world) – today. Sure, he'll talk your ear off about abstract poetry, nationalism, the importance of public intellectuals and the British Royals. But when it comes to the practical issues that affect real Canadian families – especially in a recession – he's invisible.[2]

I love that they lead their shit list with abstract poetry, like Ignatieff is Björk or the ghost of Ezra Pound. The only thing worse than poetry? *Abstract* poetry, which exists solely to make students feel stupid and professors feel smug. Then there's nationalism. Nope, can't see how that relates to governing a nation. (Silly Libs, always thinking this is a country instead of an economy!) The gratuitous monarch-bashing is odd, given that HRH is still smiling gravely from our legal tender; perhaps a right-wing plan is in the works to replace her visage with the image of an oil derrick – our one true queen and head of state.

The Cons and their ad hacks sloppily conflate two kinds of elitism. They mock Ignatieff for living in chi-chi digs in downtown Toronto instead of in the sticks or the burbs, the real Canada. He sips espresso and dips biscotti rather than sucking back double-doubles and Boston creams at the coffee dispensary of the people. Then they attack him for being a brain and a bore, for his sojourns in Yerp and at Harvard. To slam Ignatieff as "cosmopolitan" is typical right-wing nativism, divvying up the citizenry with criteria such as their proximity to livestock and dirt roads and their distance from gay bars and a decent latte. What is hilarious is seeing them mock Ignatieff's wealth and privilege. This from *Conservatives?* They love money, and the people who make lots of it.

Efforts to paint Ignatieff as a tourist, a mere visitor in his own land, play on the idea that intellectuals are always foreigners, outsiders from some theoretical fairyland. We see an even more extreme version of this notion in the Birther conspiracies that allege Obama was not born in America.

The small-town values message – on both sides of the forty-ninth parallel – is clear. Real patriots stay wherever Jesus and their mama's cooter drop 'em.

This hostility to all things foreign or urban rides shotgun with anti-intellectualism; it's all part of the same virulent reverse snobbery. Canadians and Americans express their reverse snobbery in slightly different ways, which I will return to later on when we look more closely at politics, in Chapter

Five. I'll also look at some of the differences between righty and lefty anti-intellectualism in that chapter. Republicans and the Alberta wing of Canadian politics have made exceptional contributions in the field of reverse snobbery, but they certainly do not have a monopoly on pseudo-populist poses and ideas. Democrats, Liberals, and the NDP also drop their G's, chug brewskis, and sing the praises of Joe Six-Pack. They can't attain high office without pandering to the lowest common denominator, especially when their opponents are spending so much money trying to convince the public that educated candidates are supercilious snobs.

Before we get into different flavours of anti-intellectual invective, let us look at some of the assumptions that disparate nerd-bashers share. Here is a short list of some of the most frequent allegations against the brainy.

1.   Nerds are arrogant and think they are better than you.
Nerds do not think they are better than you. Nerds *are* better than you, in their particular fields, unless you happen to be an even more devoted nerd. This is a fact. However, I must admit, as a good Canadian, that I felt quite dickish typing the phrase "better than you." North America's shared egalitarian ideals are admirable, but pseudo-populism exploits those noble notions to level the culture, to raze evidence and argument, to belittle learning so that legitimate scientific research and the myths of creationists represent "both sides of the story." A pediatrician and *Playboy* pin-up Jenny McCarthy are equally entitled to pontificate about the potential risks of vaccines. Any chump can go online and tell the world that Shakespeare

blows and those dopey books about the sparkly vampire who won't put out are the BEST EVAR!!1!!.

We have really put the duh in democracy, creating a perverse equality that entitles everyone to speak to every issue, regardless of how much they know about it. We see this on the news all the time. Ask celebrities about foreign policy, quiz the man on the street about the recession, read tweets and emails from the viewers. When a news show does invite experts to speak, producers make sure to get a batch representing "both sides" of the issue and have them squawk over each other for five barely intelligible minutes.

At the same time as the masses were being endowed with the inalienable right to rate everything on the Web or have their 140-character *pensées* voiced by CNN's Rick Sanchez, economic inequality increased and social mobility declined. The moneyed elite became more so and the cultural elite became increasingly obsolete, drowned out and washed away by a tsunami of tweets.

Becoming a nerd is hardly a viable route to the top of the social food chain when nerds are the butt of jokes, the official spokespeople for imaginary things and superannuated crud. Anyone taking classics or history for the prestige is either at Oxford or stuck in 1909. The idea that someone would get a liberal arts education to secure a perch above the lowly hordes is a misreading of current cultural conditions, given the well-worn "D'ya want fries with that?" jokes that are your reward for completing a B.A.

Conversely, people constantly use money as a form of social display. Obese SUVs, blinged-out watches, brand-name clothing, and monster homes are more flagrant and effective signifiers of one's worldly success and status than a head full of Hume or haikus. Several fields of human endeavour do a much better job of cultivating our feelings of better-than-you-ness than the long, humbling slog of study – marketing, advertising, cosmetic dentistry, and a goodly chunk of the rap industry, to name but a few.

2.   Nerds are lazy losers who expect money for nothing.

Are there lazy professors? Of course. Every occupation has its drag-ass dregs. What I take issue with is the caricature of professors as a slack species, a class of sluggards who teach a few hours a week and then get the whole summer off. School-teachers suffer from the same summers-off PR problem.

Education frequently bears the brunt of anti-public-sector sentiment. Those in the learning professions are painted as the most feckless wing of the ever-expanding civil service. This is one of the reasons why, in debates about public education, charter schools are now touted as the solution. We'll talk about them in Chapter Three, "Is Our Schools Sucking?" For the time being, suffice it to say that the appeal of charter schools is their claim to cut three things that the more-money-than-brains mindset cannot abide: government, unions, and bureaucracy.

At least schoolteachers get some sympathy for coping with your junior snot-noses and teenage hoodlums. Profs don't even get points for being glorified babysitters. And the hours we spend doing the rest of the gig – committee meetings, research, presenting conference papers, and attending university schmoozefests – are not always visible or legible to the general public, so they do not quite count as work either.

The idea that mental work is not really work is a hangover from old economies, from our days of hewing wood, drawing water, and making cars. But North America's economies are increasingly dependent on service work and office work, on the kind of labour that makes more memos, meetings, and minutes than old-fangled objects. The dematerialization of labour and the deindustrializing of the North American economy are anxiety-making social changes that have cast many workers to the winds. It's little wonder that many cling to mythic mid-twentieth-century notions about who really works for a living.

For example, shortly after Dubya began bailing out big banks and businesses, sales of Ayn Rand's *Atlas Shrugged* surged. The right-wing press read this as a sign of the Silent Majority's resistance to creeping socialism. Government growth was going to make productive people go Galt! But all of Rand's heroic capitalists triumph in industries that are now dead or bleeding. It's easy to write potboilers that posit sharp moral distinctions between the makers and the takers when you live in a big-shouldered factory world where people still make things.

The collapse of the old manufacturing economy and the growth of the new service and financial economy make Rand's ideology not just simplistic but downright nostalgic, a fantasia of a capitalism that never really was, and one that is highly unlikely to "return" soon. The producer/consumer distinction that drives her work is tough to sustain when our biggest product is consumption. It's hard to guess what that shameless elitist Howard Roark would hate more: the socialist bank bailout, the skeevy second-handing mortgage peddlers, or the miles and miles of tacky abandoned McMansions.

The Rand revival is also weird considering what happened to the world's most prominent Randian, Alan Greenspan. After years of being hailed as a guru for his outstanding achievements in the field of low, low interest rates as chairman of the Federal Reserve Board, Greenspan was hauled before Congress to explain why the markets had gone sour. He seemed unpleasantly surprised that the banking system could not rely on the virtue of selfishness as a regulatory restraint. When he was asked if his "ideology" had influenced his decisions, he admitted, "Yes, I've found a flaw. I don't know how significant or permanent it is. But I've been very distressed by that fact."

I can just picture Rand somewhere in Hell watching his testimony, eating Yankee dollars to calm her nerves as her acolyte apologized to the ultimate second-handers, those bureaucratic leeches and appropriators. (Ayn is doubly horrified when she realizes she is eating – *aaargh* – rubles. This *is* Hell!)

I digress. The main point is that academia is not the leisurely ivied stroll it is rumoured to be. If anything, a weak academic job market has made everyone but the exceptionally fortunate work much harder and has engendered the kind of competition, red in tooth and claw, that free marketeers always praise. *Money for nothing* is a much more accurate description of cashing in on swelling Internet stocks or soaring house prices. People love money for nothing! That's why the lotto is so successful. That's why Greenspan was hailed as a genius for making money as cheap as borscht. It's money for thinking – which looks suspiciously like nothing – that the public seems to object to.

3. Nerds are social engineers who want to tell everyone what to do.

The only thing worse than a slothful prof is a bossy one. Intellectuals are always itching to advise, to embroil the public in diabolical social experiments. Daycare, gay rights, multiculturalism, and women working are good examples of the sort of social change the right thinks that nerds have engineered. Lefty allegations of evil egghead meddling point to things like cubic or part-fish tomatoes, weapons manufacturing, Big Pharma, and global trade agreements.

Different political groups, on the right and the left, often share a key presupposition: experts want to control you, thus expertise itself is a sinister force. Moreover, both agree that so-called experts only mess up the natural order of things. For example, conservatives contend that activist judges ruined heterosexual marriage with 2.3 kids, while lefties argue that Monsanto's chemists wrecked gnarly local veggies grown in genuine organic manure.

In *Anti-intellectualism in American Life*, Richard Hofstader argues that the public increasingly distrust expertise precisely because they have become so dependent on it. As American society became more complex and highly organized after the world wars, the power of the experts grew, and people became increasingly nervous about their activities and proclivities, their sway over society. Complexity, Hofstader says, has "steadily whittled away the functions the ordinary citizen can intelligently and comprehendingly perform for himself."[3]

North American society has continued to become more complex, more technologically sophisticated, since Hofstader wrote these words nearly fifty years ago, in the early days of the TV age. We now rely on new experts, such as the programmers who keep our online banking sites up and running. Technology may make us feel like we are performing more functions for ourselves – pay bills in your jammies with the click of a mouse! – but comprehension fails many of us when the site or modem crashes. All those easy-to-navigate web pages are floating on an unseen sea of technical expertise.

Lack of computer savvy is just the tip of the not-knowing, of the systems we depend on that stretch beyond our individual ken. The more complex shit gets, the more we are engulfed by structures we do not and cannot comprehend, the more anxious we get about our understanding of the world and suck on our soggy, well-gnawed ideological binkies.

This is why explanations such as "intellectual elites ruined everything" are so appealing. They order apparently chaotic events and turn them into familiar stories of good versus evil. The big problem with this particular tale is that it credits nerds with positively super-villainous powers and plans. *After we destroy traditional values, we shall repair to our mountain hideaway and turn on the Weather Machine!* The mad scientist and the loony prof are hardy pop-culture stereotypes. But they are also alive and well in political life and public discourse, where brains get the blame for social changes that come from a confluence of political and economic causes.

4. Nerds have never run anything real and they live in a candy-coloured dream world.

It seems silly to dispute the existence of schools. We've all seen them, and the vast majority of us have attended one or more. Nevertheless, the academic realm is not just excluded from the real world but pitted against it, described as its opposite, as if it does not properly exist. This opposition between school and the real, between learning and doing, does students a great disservice by sending them the mixed message that school is very important, but most of the stuff you learn there is not!

So cram, cheat, pass, and forget. Binge and purge info when required, then advance to the next level and the next until you reach the end screen of graduation and enter regularly scheduled reality, already in progress. It's okay to game the system when the system is a game. You jump through hoops so employers know you can jump through hoops; nobody gives a shit whether you majored in regular hoops, flaming hoops, or jumping and juggling at the same time.

A number of post-secondary institutions, ranging from accredited universities to substandard diploma mills, try to pitch themselves as education for the "real world," which perpetuates the notion that campuses are spun of fairy dust and wishes. This split between academia and reality is based on the popular conception of thought and action as polar opposites. Thinking is not the necessary precursor to action, or simply another kind of activity. Instead, thought is the enemy of efficacy and resolve, a perilously querulous anti-productive drag. Doubt is the mark of the quisling. Deliberation is flip-flopping or waffling, failure or unwillingness to heed the call of the heart and the gut. Consideration equals procrastination. Perspiration trumps contemplation.

This sense that activity is real and thinking is artificial is not confined to either side of the political aisle. The right wing's dismissal of academia as unreal may be more straight-forward and full-throated, but the activist left is equally hostile towards tenured stooges who sit in cushy offices writing about poor people's problems in elite, specialized jargon poor people cannot read.

Others who appoint themselves arbiters of the real do so from a perspective that pleads political neutrality, that speaks for the common sense that politicians and professors of all stripes have abjured. These denizens of the real world, such as business owners, managers, lobbyists, and pundits, are qualified to call for the demise of fields they know nothing about precisely because they know nothing about them. Here ignorance functions as proof of their savvy, a sign that Mr. or Ms. Real World is too sharp to be hornswoggled by some fraudulent, futile major like literature, history, philosophy, or women's studies.

Occasionally Mr. Real World will cap his argument by insisting that he has read the compleat works of Lofty Classic on his own time, to unwind from the rigours of reality. If he can do some poncy English major's alleged job on evenings and weekends, it is hardly real work. Culture may well be elevating and all – that's why he reads Lofty Classic instead of the trash his office mates prefer – but it remains secondary and adjacent to the real world.

We can surmise from such speeches what is not real. The real world is not made of words or art or the past or idealistic theories about equality. Where is this real world and what is it made of? Most people who use the phrase "the real world" are referring to entities like the economy and jobs and money. That makes this particular tenet of reverse snobbery absurd. What newspaper have they been reading throughout the crashes and recessions of the past few years? The *Pie-Eyed Optimist Times?* The *Hooray for Everything Herald Tribune?*

Economic turbulence causes real suffering. At the same time, though, it is loopy to deny that vast tracts of modern capitalism are notional, speculative, crazy-brilliant conceptual constructs made up of digital bits and jargon and math that are every bit as imaginary and actual as Hamlet. The word *real* has been besmirched by prefixes such as "keepin' it" and suffixes like "-ity TV." When it appears between *the* and *world,* it becomes a rhetorical cudgel, a club to clobber thinking that has no immediate practical value – or at least none that Mr. or Ms. Real World can ascertain.

5. Nerds are living in the past, hung up on defunct ideas.
We often point to our magnificent technological achievements as evidence of our triumph over those benighted primitives who preceded us. I definitely get this vibe from my students. "Why do we need to read this old stuff?" they grouse. It's, like, *old,* from the back-in-the-day times when

people shat in buckets and were too stupid to invent cool stuff like cellphones. The past is just one long, smelly error until we get to the car, computer, and iPod.

Anything that happened before the students were born is part of the same undifferentiated mass. Sporadically the void spits up costume movies and video games that make youngsters hazily aware of periods such as the toga times and the era of men in silly wigs and skin-tight breeches. Much of their historical knowledge is actually pop-cultural. They recognize evil Nazis and surly, embittered Vietnam vets from Oscar-bait and action movies and games like *Call of Duty*. But they do not have a very robust sense of when things happened, or what came before them.

Sometimes this ignorance of history expresses itself in the form of backhanded compliments. My English undergrads seem surprised when something old turns out to be interesting. Even though we have much better scary things now, like the *Saw* franchise, Poe is not boring – or at least not as boring as *Macbeth*. They cannot quite believe that a rickety claptrap machine like "The Tell-Tale Heart" still functions in spite of its advanced age. And nineteenth-century lit is not really even old in nerd years.

This notion is a testament to the way that technical and economic reasoning elbow out other ways of thinking and dominate student expectations, regardless of their major. If it's new, it's more likely to be true and to falsify or negate whatever came before. Reading-intensive subjects such as literature and philosophy, and history itself, suffer under this paradigm, since books and lectures have become antiquated knowledge-delivery systems, consigned to the scrap heap by the predigested info globs of PowerPoint slide shows.

Retention is being outsourced to our prosthetic brains. Why clog your head with tedious facts about the past when you can simply demand an exam review sheet or consult Google or Wikipedia? But there's something else at work here too. I remember prodding one particularly inert group of undergraduate dial tones thus: "I get the sense that you guys aren't really interested in what people two hundred years ago thought." They shrugged. No, not really, was the classroom consensus. What the hell did it have to do with them?

We see a similar shrugging in public life. In a 2009 appearance on HBO's *Real Time with Bill Maher,* Republican Meghan McCain declared, "I wouldn't know; I wasn't born yet,"[4] when Democratic strategist Paul Begala mentioned the way Reagan had blamed many of his problems on Carter. Another prominent Republican blonde, former White House press secretary Dana Perino, displayed the same whatevs attitude in 2007. In a press conference she dodged a question comparing Bush's policy to Kennedy's handling of the Cuban missile crisis. Later, on an NPR quiz show, Perino admitted, "I was panicked a bit because I really don't know about . . . the Cuban missile crisis . . . It had to do with Cuba and missiles, I'm pretty sure."[5]

How could she know? Perino is a pup. She was born in 1972, a decade after the 1962 U.S.-Soviet nuclear showdown. It's not like she was there.

This Young Earth thinking – I am Year Zero! – obliterates history. Meghan McCain and my bored students are essentially Whig historians who do not know what the term *Whig*

history means. They think that they live in the best of all possible worlds and act as though all previous generations were
just eejits, fumbling and bumbling their way towards the
world we live in now, where everyone knows better. Consequently, they are free to ignore the past. This is sad, and scary,
because it means they are like goldfish in a bowl, totally
trapped in their own cultural moment, unable to consider it
critically or compare it to anything.

6.   Nerds are negative nellies: pessimists and player-haters.
The only kind of thinking that sells really well is positive
thinking. Unfortunately, this is not thinking at all. For example,
The Secret book and DVD both did gangbusters. Those who
market *The Secret* and hawk its law of attraction maintain
that "it is the culmination of many centuries of great thinkers,
scientists, artists and philosophers."[6] But I'm quite confident
that both Jesus and Leonardo da Vinci had a more challenging and complicated world view than "wishing extra-hard
makes it so," which is what the gurus of *The Secret* teach their
terminally credulous followers.

In a similar vein, many of the most successful megachurches of recent years retail prosperity gospels, reassuring
you that Jesus wants you to be rich, that you are all (to filch a
phrase from the troublingly toothy Joel Osteen) "God's mas-
terpiece." Never mind that Christ's instructions to would-be
followers are quite explicit, right there in the Bible in red type:
yard sale, drain the accounts, give it all away, and get back to
me when I know you really mean it. Some of the most popular
strains of contemporary Christianity have more to say about

getting than giving, casting the Lord as a celestial career coach and concierge and the priest or minister as a – gross portmanteau alert – pastorpreneur.

In a 2008 *New York Times* op ed, writer Barbara Ehrenreich linked the popularity of New Agey and Christianish positive thinking to the mortgage meltdown. She wrote:

> The idea is [that] . . . thinking things, "visualizing" them – ardently and with concentration – actually makes them happen. You will be able to pay that adjustable rate mortgage or, at the other end of the transaction, turn thousands of bad mortgages into giga-profits, the reasoning goes, if only you truly believe that you can.[7]

All that complicated fiscal math was a towering cathedral of logic tottering on a squidgy foundation of feelings. John Maynard Keynes used the term *animal spirits* to describe the psychological or emotional underpinnings of the market, such as trust and confidence. The Internet and housing bubbles of the past twenty years were periods of overconfidence, of investors getting skunk-drunk on optimism. The crashes and slumps of 2000, 2008, and 2009 were the hangover and morning-after regrets as hot dot-coms and formerly foxy mortgages proved coyote ugly in the merciless morning sun.

Our valorization of belief, our conviction that faith and certitude are virtues, makes the hard work of thinking look pretty dour in comparison. Doubt, skepticism, research, revision, sustained criticism: all of these read as negative, which is a big cultural no-no. Staying positive in spite of the odds, in spite of the facts, is lauded as beneficial to our physical and spiritual health and our capacity to accumulate wealth.

Rational thought has become an excluded middle, squished and muffled by more popular mental modes such as wishing and counting. The practical, money-minded side dismisses thinking as useless navel-gazing, and the wishful one sees it as a major downer, bad thoughts that beckon bad news. Criticizing is just complaining – another object of bipartisan scorn. The right contends that lefty criticisms of markets or the latest war are blame-America-firsting, the mewling and puling of moon-bat losers who are jealous of the successes of suits and soldiers. At the other end of the ideological spectrum from these beefy pragmatists, the flaky and wishful also take a dim view of criticism. They decry negative energy and channelling too much of one's vital force into corrosive pessimism, lest one poison oneself with hatred.

Even though these two camps appear to have little in common, they both contend that criticism is a wholly personal matter. This is another sign of the decline of reasonable argument; objections are routinely reduced to personal or private squabbles, expressions of petty passions such as jealousy or bitterness. Cons attribute liberal gripes to the individual whinger's envy or thwarted longing to be the boss of everyone. New Agers exhort us to let go of the unhappy thoughts, as focusing on them will curdle our spirit. In both cases, it is actually all about you: narcissism in the guise of traditional morality or the latest spirituality.

The rugged-individualist and hippy-trippy versions of

pro-positive rhetoric both sound awfully retrograde to me. Complaints about complaining, no matter their political slant, all tell us the same thing: Shut up and smile, smile, smile. Keep a gratitude journal, churls. You can thank your executive liege lords for the gift of unpaid overtime and your daily ladlefuls of high-fructose corn gruel.

This complaint – that nerds are negative – is not as goofy or paranoid as the preceding five. Professors can appear negative when they debunk some cherished notion or drop more bad news about our expanding debts, waistlines, and environmental wreckage. But this is one of the most valuable public services nerds provide. Negativity and pessimism are seriously – maybe even dangerously – underrated in North America.

Astute readers have doubtless noticed that these six complaints about nerds contradict each other. But intrepid anti-intellectuals continue to combine them, jumping from charge to charge in the space of a single op ed, speech, sentence, or protest sign. Can someone please let me know if we're supposed to be lazy losers who can't hack it in the real world, or corrupters of youth, enemies of capital, and despoilers of democracy? I'd like to adjust my alarm clock accordingly.

This kind of cognitive dissonance is not a problem if you deny that cogitation has value, if you insist that feelings and beliefs are more authentic, more democratic, more trustworthy than ideas. The realm of feelings and beliefs is much more accommodating than reason or history, allowing nerd-bashers to posit a world where intellectuals are simultaneously ineffectual and threatening, buffoons and tempters, failures at life and the covert masters of the world.

Public discourse is a messy mélange of bean-counting, belligerence, and bathos, of number crunching and emoting. We veer from childish wishes (house prices will go up forever!) and hysterical declarations to narrow calculations and reductive analyses. Just watch your local news team as they whipsaw between raw numbers (box-office totals, the GDP, unemployment rates, grim health stat o' the day) and ploys to jerk tears, fear, and *aaw*s from their audience (house fire, terrorists, child abduction, kid eats ice cream). Numbers and stats bob in a sentimental slop, a swampy slurry of bits of hard data and buckets of mushy manipulation.

Education might look like one of the most centrist issues possible, given that virtually everyone, from wealthy employers to impecunious hippies, agrees that kids should be well-educated. Even the most boorish politician knows better than to run on a platform of fewer, crappier schools and lazier, thicker children. But this nice warm unanimity dissipates quickly when we start talking about why we need good schools, what we mean by good schools, and how we might improve schools.

Arguments about schools and universities, and the way we conduct those arguments, show us that the North American public is quite riven about the life of the mind. We may be dismissive of intellectual life, but we are also exceedingly defensive about it. We are quite anxious about our collective intelligence, constantly fretting about the better students of worse lands supplanting our slack little button-mashing screen junkies.

Again, though, this concern has more to do with money than brains. We're not worried that our kids will be less well-read than Chinese students. Instead we fear that they will lose out economically and technologically, that the flow of shit work will turn against us and we will be stuck making the poisonous toys and tainted toothpaste, horror of horrors. This is why there are campaigns to get more kids to study the STEM disciplines: science, tech, engineering, and math.

Of course these subjects are important; even Mr. and Ms. Real World will condone them. But it's foolish and counterproductive to insist that these are the only subjects that really matter and that we should starve the spendthrift arts to save the sciences. First, this ignores the economy of most post-secondary institutions. Science students require a panoply of expensive equipment, which is subsidized by el cheapo arts majors. Pricey instructional tech is slowly creeping into the liberal arts, but the majority of humanities classes require nothing more than a room and a prof and a pile of books.

If that prof is an adjunct – and many in the liberal arts are – the labour costs for the class are less than a single student's tuition fee. The other twenty-nine, forty-nine, or ninety-nine cheques are free to fund the more important functions and tools of the modern university: new computers for the geeks, feeding the protective blubbery layers of administrators and fundraisers, and splashing out for marketing baubles like snazzier dorms and shinier brochures and websites.

Second, pushing kids who have no interest in a topic to study it as a means to an end guarantees that there will be a goodly number of incompetent, resentful dullards drawing blood and drafting blueprints in the near future. And that's if they last that long, gritting their teeth and sticking it out till graduation. Nearly half of the people who start a college degree in the U.S.A. never finish it. Steering someone towards a particular major is too little, too late. Cultivating quality nerds is a process that has to start much earlier.

When employers bitch and moan about college grads – can't read, can't write, stare blankly when you mention the before-times – their complaints suggest that liberal-artsy skills such as general knowledge and linguistic ability do have some use after all. But a rigorous humanities education also teaches you that there are values other than use, that there is more to human existence than being an employee busy brown-nosing or, better yet, becoming the boss.

Our insistence that everything, especially education, need be useful is wrong-headed. The presumption that everything exists merely for our use is spectacularly ignorant and wantonly destructive, and it's partly responsible for our ongoing and intertwined economic and environmental difficulties. Moreover, the idea that we are hard-nosed pragmatists, that North Americans venerate usefulness above all things, is utterly at odds with all that crazy shit we've just bought and hope to replace and upgrade someday soon, when this whole recession/depression thing finally blows over.

Every university offers a couple of courses that sound kooky and easy to mock in an op ed. But have you been in a

Wal-Mart or on Amazon.com lately? How much of that junk is, strictly speaking, useful? It's pretty hilarious that a culture so devoted to toys and divertissements and status symbols and paraprofessions and pseudo-sciences pitches hissy fits about usefulness when students are wasting their time and money on literature, history, and philosophy. No, it's far better for them to drop out and pursue a higher calling, like popularizing another cheap piece of plastic guaranteed to delight and serve for mere minutes before it clogs landfills from here to eternity. If they must learn, they should study something really real, something with lots of rote memorizing and right or wrong answers, or the latest trendy, tradesy e-degree. Hell, then they can come up with something truly useful, like a new iFart application.

Throughout this book, I will look at the way our more-money-than-brains mindset affects schools, universities, politics, and pop culture. First, though, a caveat: one of the risks of writing a book like this is the "get off my lawn" tone that creeps into conversations about ignorance and anti-intellectualism. Teachers have bitched about the kids today since Socrates and Saint Augustine bemoaned their feckless charges. Every generation seems to turn declinist when it starts to sag and flag. I would like to avoid this kind of *argumentum ad fogeyum.*

First, it is unfair to all the great students I've had, smart kids of all ages who still care about reading and thinking. Second, I can't really make a proper declinist argument – one that traces a drop-off from a high point. At the risk of sounding Meghan McCainish, I was born after the periods that other cultural critics cite as periods of intellectual verve and pro-nerd sentiment, such as Hofstader's early 1960s.

I'm not really interested in pursuing the gap between our particular cultural moment and some wiser age, anyway. It's not like we can hop in the way-back machine and pretend away developments such as the cable spectrum or the Web, nor would I want to do so. The Internet can be an invaluable resource. There are plenty of intelligent blogs and even more plum dumb books. No medium has the monopoly on bad ideas. Explanations that heap all the blame on text messaging or video games and rap are no better than fulminations against the intellectual elite.

I'm not worried about our failing to live up to the past, though it is a bummer to see so many blithely forget it. This is a really teachery thing to say, but North America's problem is that it is not living up to its potential. What interests me is the gap between our speeches about schools and the actual school system. What interests me is the gap between North America's technical sophistication and our ignorance and intolerance of other branches of knowledge.

Pandering to the common folks and their simple ways is the brightly coloured cultural candy-coating on the bitter pill of policies that are anything but populist. Sarah Palin, who has enjoyed a six-figure income for some time, plays working-class heroine by serving moose chili with a side of word salad. She swings the real-world cudgel with indefatigable vim. I'm sure she believes every garbled word, but her white-trash minstrel show in fact equates being working class with being an ignoramus.

Palin's popularity is a perfect example of the way class has been divorced from wealth and is now wedded to cultural signifiers like religion, rhetoric, and hobbies. People born to trust-fundom and the beneficiaries of the past few bubbles – members of the loftiest economic classes – are not the elite. Rather, the elitists are the ones who sound like they've spent too much time in class. A delightful example of this occurred when Lady de Rothschild, a mogul and Clinton fundraiser, decamped to the McCain campaign because she feared that Barack Obama was an elitist. In an interview with CNN's Wolf Blitzer, she said it was so sad to see the Democratic Party "play the class card," and then ended by alleging that Blitzer was the elitist, not her.[8]

I reckon that Wolf makes a pretty penny for being on CNN whenever Larry King and Anderson Cooper aren't. Still, his talking-head salary likely approximates the fresh flower budget for the de Rothschild family estates. But Blitzer is part of the media and de Rothschild, the humble daughter of an aviation company owner in Jersey, just happened to make a pile and marry into a family synonymous with wealth. She is an ordinary self-made millionaire aristocrat who wants to live in an America where anybody – nay, everybody! – can be an ordinary self-made millionaire aristocrat too.

The anti-elitist invective against nerds is laughable when you consider its sources. It is quite a feat of magician's misdirection, a depressingly effective conjuring of pointy-headed straw men and scarecrows. One of the brutal truths of anti-intellectualism, or at least the version that currently prevails, is that it does not harm intellectuals that much. Oh sure, the name-calling, the snarky op eds, and the budget cuts sting. Job losses and ill-paid part-time gigs – all the rage lately in ostensibly elite fields such as journalism and academia – are difficult to bear. The acquaintances and relatives disappointed that you are not a "real" doctor can also be a swift kick in the ego.

These insults and indignities are flesh wounds compared to the damage that anti-intellectualism inflicts on some of the groups that embrace it ardently, that defend their ignorance as a virtue, be they the too-cool-for-school kids who inadvertently consign themselves to lives of poverty and drudgery or the electorates that must endure policies enacted by plutocratic pols playing just plain folks in order to pick their pockets.

Jeremiads against the nerd elite play on our egalitarian sympathies, but they seem misplaced and daffy given the obeisance we render to other, much more powerful elites. Anti-intellectualism and ignorance have crummy socio-economic consequences, and they do some serious ethical damage too. Institutions such as the free press, democracy, and free markets collapse into farragoes of corruption and incompetence without the scrutiny of an informed populace. Notions such as universal suffrage and inalienable human rights are inextricably linked to the idea of universal human reason, the sense that we are all thinking people who can disagree and debate matters without resorting to fisticuffs or deadly force. When we valorize ignorance and debase reason, we diminish man and the humanity that dwells within him, to bum an old-fashioned phrase from Kant.

Chapter Two

AT THE ARSE END OF THE LATE, GREAT ENLIGHTENMENT

—

The motto of Enlightenment is therefore: Sapere aude! *Have courage to use your own understanding! Laziness and cowardice are the reasons why such a large proportion of men, even when nature has long emancipated them from alien guidance nevertheless gladly remain immature for life. For the same reasons, it is all too easy for others to set themselves up as their guardians. It is so convenient to be immature!*

— IMMANUEL KANT[1]

In the summer of 2009, Fox News bloviator Glenn Beck embarked on his "Common Sense Comedy Tour," a title that contains precisely one accurate descriptor. Beck, a dry-drunk Mormon shock jock, dressed in Founding Fathers regalia accessorized with a pair of sneakers. Beck said that he wore the eighteenth-century costume to illustrate that the founders were regular folk, just like the lumpenyanks in the audience. Oh sure, they might have been geniuses, Beck concedes, but they couldn't come up with deodorant or pockets, haw haw haw. The Enlightenment luminaries who wrote America's founding documents were not that different from them. They loooved their country and stood up for it. Were the good people in the crowd willing to do the same – to rise up and resist the threat of out-of-control government?

This is one of Beck's favourite themes. The audience in the video I watched applauded and hooted when he hollered, voice cracking with fury, that the people in Washington had no right to tell them what to do, or to tell their school district what to do. His fans appear to be firm believers in the myth that nerds are social engineers who want to run everything. They also dig the notion that complexity is an elitist lie. Beck got big yuks for poking fun at the thousand-page climate-change bill. Why, that's longer than the New Testament. "The government's attempt to try to control the weather was longer than the story of the guy who actually could control the weather!" Beck yelped, to claps, whoops, and *yeah!*s.

Beck uses the tag line "the Fusion of Enlightenment and Entertainment" to plug his radio, TV, book, and Web empire. Like Bill O'Reilly before him, he claims to operate outside the Republican machine, styling himself as a libertarian. But that is not what distinguishes Beck from compeers such as Rush Limbaugh and O'Reilly. Beck blows his stack like O'Reilly and he does nyah-nyah voice mockery like Limbaugh, but he has added some new elements to the mix: hysterical blubbering and over-the-top emoting. He loooves his country so much that his eyeballs runneth over.

I hope that Thomas Paine, wherever his righteous radical shade may be, cannot see the affairs of this world. That noble rabble-rouser should be spared the indignity of seeing this bawling clown, this yowling toddler, slobbering all over him. Referring to *Common Sense*, Paine's genuinely revolutionary tract, allows Beck to market his reactionary, reductive opinions as risky anti-government rebellion. In the book that accompanies his Common Sense Comedy Tour, *Glenn Beck's Common Sense*, he brags, "The fastest way to be branded a danger, a militia member or just plain crazy is to quote the words of our Founding Fathers."[2]

Ooh-hoo-hoo! This must be the comedy part of his act. Yes, Glenn, you sure are threatening the system, sticking it to the man with your top-rated cable show, radio show, and *New York Times* bestsellers. Paine did hard time and suffered harsh treatment for his ideas. Beck isn't even willing to wear period shoes for the cause of prop comedy.

I hate to see perfectly good ideas get swallowed, sucked into the bilious goo that sloshes inside Beck's grossly distended brand. With friends like this guy, the Enlightenment does not need enemies. But it has lots of those too. Funny thing, though: even those enemies, the folks who claim to hate Enlightenment ideals, still use their language to make a case for their right to oppose them.

Consider, for example, the way many in the intelligent-design camp defend their position. Stumping for his odious documentary *Expelled: No Intelligence Allowed*, Ben Stein argued that those who oppose creationism in the classroom are squelchers of free inquiry, politicizers befouling the objectivity of scientific research. This is one of the most common

God-botherer gambits: to demand that the enlightened virtue of tolerance must encompass their intolerance.

Are persistent appeals to Enlightenment ideals evidence of their robust health? Would that it were so. We pay lip service to freedom and reason but we repeatedly backslide into good ol' superstition, credulity, and authoritarianism, the enemies of enlightenment. Religious and fiscal fundamentalism, rigid political ideologies, and the immaturity lionized by mass culture compromise our ability and willingness to exercise our most fundamental freedoms.

The end of the Enlightenment meme has been bouncing around the scientific community and the press for the past few years. The *New Scientist* ran a story on its demise in 2005, wondering why so many people are so hell-bent on "rejecting reason, tolerance and freedom of thought."[3] Several op eds in major newspapers have declared that reason and freedom have joined the choir invisible. George Monbiot and Garry Wills wrote the lefty-liberal versions of this eulogy. Monbiot pointed to the crackdown on civil liberties after 9/11, and Wills worried that Dubya's re-election was a sign that Americans did not really care for reason or science.[4] Victor Davis Hanson delivered a right-wing version of this rant, arguing that Europeans and American leftists were betraying their noble Enlightenment heritage and wimping out of the war for modern freedom – the war against barbarous Islam.[5]

The end of the Enlightenment is one of those bipartisan declinisms. Libs bemoan censorship, the Patriot Act, and creationism as evidence of our diminished commitment to freedom and rationality. Cons crab about political correctness, market regulation, and the cult of global warming, citing similar concerns about freedom. The issues and culprits differ but the substance of these complaints is comparable: too much arbitrary authority, too many babies trying to dodge certain truths, comporting themselves like spoiled brats.

This is also the complaint we hear in the Kant quote that opens this chapter, lines from one of the most oft-cited examples of Enlightenment thinking, his short essay "Answering the Question: What Is Enlightenment?" For Kant, being enlightened means being a grown-up. Those countries, cultures, and individuals that remain dependent on "alien guidance" are still stuck in the ignorance and irresponsibility of childhood, sucking up to Big Dad. He goes on to say:

> If I have a book to serve as my understanding, a pastor to serve as my conscience, a physician to determine my diet for me, and so on, I need not exert myself at all. I need not think, if only I can pay: others will readily undertake the irksome work for me.

That, friends, is one daisy-fresh eighteenth-century bitch-slap. It effectively indicts half of the current best-seller list, taking out most of the self-help, spirituality, and diet tomes. It spanks the televangelical hucksters who promise blessings – including cash – in exchange for cash. It clips Oprah, at least half of her guests, and her hideous progeny Dr. Phil. It's the sort of sentiment that makes me think the Enlightenment is worth revisiting.

Scholars quibble about when the Enlightenment began and ended, but many nerds have agreed on a long eighteenth century, one that starts around 1660 and ends in 1830, encompassing events such as the Glorious (British), American, and French revolutions and luminaries such as John Locke, David Hume, Adam Smith, Voltaire, Denis Diderot, and Immanuel Kant. Whichever way you bracket the period, the United States and Canada are its children.

You can see our dependence on this Enlightenment legacy in the things we brag about when we brag about our countries. We also turn to its terms when the going gets rough, huffing and puffing on the fumes of the Age of Reason whenever we need words and values to define and defend ourselves. After 9/11 and throughout the War on Terror, there was a lot of Enlightenment-flavoured talk, a succession of speeches from U.S. administration officials and Canadian leaders underlining the importance of freedom and democracy and insisting that the freedoms North Americans enjoy are universal human rights.

It is *echt* Enlightenment to insist upon the universal character of freedom and reason, to argue that men should be autonomous self-governors. It may have taken the social movements of the intervening centuries to extend that definition of *man* to include broke men, women, and non-honkies, but this idea of human freedom is a legacy of the eighteenth century.

It's reductive to boil down a big cosmopolitan pan-national period into a single Enlightenment project or program, and that is not my intention. But this chapter, being brief, will necessarily involve a little philosophical violence and some summary takes. Nor am I cheerleading for reason. There are legitimate criticisms of the Enlightenment, cautionary polemics about the dangers of reason and science turning into dogmatic rationalism and scientism.

In their 1944 book *Dialectic of Enlightenment,* Max Horkheimer and Theodor Adorno begin by asserting that the "wholly enlightened earth is radiant with triumphant calamity"[6] as the utopian schemes of the nineteenth century culminated in the totalitarian slaughter-benches of the twentieth. They argue that, for the Enlightenment, "anything which does not conform to the standard of calculability or utility must be viewed with suspicion." This is worth underlining, because the part of the Enlightenment legacy that Horkheimer and Adorno criticize at length is also the part that remains most vital for us. We are exceedingly enthusiastic about quantification and technological advancement. The idea that knowledge is a way of mastering nature is deeply ingrained in our culture.

Consider how we discuss global warming. Those who deny or oppose doing anything about climate change occupy a position that simultaneously endorses our mastery over nature and shrugs it away. They argue that we are actually subject to nature (or God), but only so they can conclude that it is stupid to blame ourselves for the freaky weather. We can and must cheerfully continue exploiting nature, since our complex modern economies and comfy lifestyles depend on this dominion. To do otherwise is to deny the glorious march of progress.

Those who favour action against global warming also accept the premise that we are masters of nature, but they argue that we are very bad ones indeed, and must move from dominion to stewardship. Both factions – the environmentalists and the righties who oppose environmentalism – are working two sides of the same Enlightenment coin. They also accuse each other of being anti-enlightened: climate-change deniers are against science, and greens are against modernity, or so go the slurs.

Our mania for quantification and utility affects every sphere of human endeavour, even the artsy ones. Movies are judged by their special effects budgets or box-office totals, humanities professorships are determined by how many articles the candidate has managed to publish, and the press is simply nutty for listicles and star ratings, which are ways of converting culture into easily telegraphed quanta.

But utility and technology were not really ends in themselves for most Enlightenment thinkers, as they often are for many of us. For them, things like science and markets mattered because they contribute to human freedom. Here are some of the defining characteristics of that freedom.

Theological freedom, or freedom of conscience

The Protestants inaugurated the notion that we do not need any fancy-schmancy pope or bejewelled ecclesiastical hierarchy to mediate the relationship between man and God. Lamentably, that Lutheran brainwave also sparked years and years of brutal religious warfare. Then and now, the Enlightenment call for secular states or for the separation of

Church and State is an attempt to halt such internecine blood-shed and to recognize that divisions in Christianity mean we can no longer live in states governed by a single dogma.

Enlightenment thought is not totally godless. But it isn't Christian the way Glenn Beckheads claim it is, either. Many Enlightenment thinkers believed in a hands-off deist god, one we could see at work in nature. And some of them objected to religious dogma and clerical power precisely because they spread coercive, divisive religious precepts that corrupt rational or natural religion. Locke says as much in his "Letter on Toleration." Thomas Paine offers a much more radical version of this argument in his *Age of Reason,* where he writes:

> I do not believe in the creed professed by the Jewish church, by the Roman church, by the Greek church, by the Turkish church, by the Protestant church, nor by any church that I know of. My own mind is my own church.
>
> All national institutions of churches, whether Jewish, Christian, or Turkish, appear to me no other than human inventions, set up to terrify and enslave mankind, and monopolize power and profit.
>
> I do not mean by this declaration to condemn those who believe otherwise; they have the same right to their belief as I have to mine.[7]

That final caveat is very important. Paine may reject institutionalized religion in the strongest possible terms, but he also maintains that we all have the right to our own beliefs, provided that those beliefs do not transgress or suppress others' freedom of conscience.

Religion becomes a problem when it tries to curb rational inquiry, which is a God-given inclination, right, and responsibility. Scripture, or a particular faith's interpretation of it, cannot serve as a substitute for individual, independent thought and conscience. Kant is certainly no atheist, but he cautions us that being good out of fear or to curry eternal favour is actually immature and immoral, another instance of our desire to be bossed and dandled by Big Dad.

The relationship between religion and politics is one of the significant differences between Americans and Canadians, one that helps account for Canada's liberal policies with respect to issues such as gay marriage and abortion. The U.S. was settled by Puritans, and it remains the most fervently religious country in the developed world. Canada was founded by a mishmash of Loyalists, *coureurs de bois*, and dirt farmers. Some of them were every bit as devout as their southern neighbours, but Canada's long, proud tradition of squelching public displays of zeal has discouraged the theopolitical proselytizing that is so prominent in American politics. Twice as many Americans as Canadians regularly attend church, and Americans are much more likely to say that their private faith influences their political choices.

This is not surprising, but some of their beliefs are. In the year of Our Lord 2000, the Southern Baptist Convention agreed upon the following:

The Holy Bible was written by men divinely inspired and is God's revelation of Himself to man. It is a perfect treasure of divine instruction. It has God for its author, salvation for its end, and truth, without any mixture of error, for its matter. Therefore, all Scripture is totally true and trustworthy.[8]

This sort of Biblical literalism is not merely a pre-modern position but a pre-medieval one, since theologians as early as Saint Augustine argued for an allegorical reading of the Bible. This puts the Southern Baptist Convention and its co-religionists on the other side of 397 AD. They are not goofing around when they sing "Gimme that old-time religion."

It is also odd when religion uses the latest heathen innovations in the service of the totally true and trustworthy. The American Creation Museum, which opened in Petersburg, Kentucky, in May 2007, is a state-of-the-art multi-million-dollar facility with more than a hundred displays, a planetarium, and a couple of theatres. Here you can watch "Children play and dinosaurs roam near Eden's Rivers," thanks to high-tech exhibits engineered by a former designer for Universal Studios.[9]

The Creation Museum is a sign of the times, the perfect image of an age that is simultaneously complex and cloddish, sophisticated and wilfully stunned. Museums grew out of the Enlightenment belief in universal knowledge. They were encyclopedias you could walk through, places where you could commune with the seemingly infinite diversity of human reason.

The Creation Museum explicitly repudiates the Enlightenment at the same time that it shamelessly rips it off. It employs the tropes of reason and science to lay waste to reason and science, using modern technology to dismiss the kind of inquiry that made such tools possible. The museum's website boasts, "Our halls are gilded with truth." It's a felicitous verb choice, since *gilding* means applying a thin veneer, a surface coat of gold atop the inferior bulk beneath.

There are some thickets of Bible-thumpery here in the Great White North, and they have been emboldened by the success of their southern fellows. There is a Creation Science Museum in Big Valley, Alberta, that uses the wealth of local fossils to conjure up visions of dinosaurs on Noah's ark. However, it is open only by appointment and housed in a modest bungalow that looks like a retiree's house, save for the dinosaur replica perched above the door, a gargoyle warding off the demons of secular humanism.

Of course, it would be overstating the case to say that religion is simply a stupefying force. For much of history, churches, synagogues, temples, and mosques were essential to the preservation and production of texts, which means it's hard to go deep into old literature or history without paying attention to sacred works. And studying the Bible, old-timey theology, and other religious traditions is a really good way to combat dunderheaded fundie proselytizing. Good luck launching comparative religion classes in the Bible belt, though; what can possibly compare to the totally true and trustworthy?

Most mainstream Protestant and Catholic denominations tend to let Jesus and Darwin co-exist as different explanations for different registers of existence. Parents and preachers who cannot abide this milquetoast moderate position keep trying to drive Darwin and his devilish apes out of their blessed broods' schools. U.S. courts have repeatedly ruled that classes that give "equal time" to creation science and actual science are unconstitutional. Nevertheless, plucky believers in states such as Kansas, Ohio, and Pennsylvania have soldiered on.

In 2009 the Alberta legislature passed a law granting parents the right to pull their young 'uns out of classes covering hot topics like religion, sex, and sexual orientation. School boards now have to notify parents about impending classes with a high risk of secular hedonism. One MLA, Rob Anderson, said that there were "thousands and thousands of parents, the silent majority, severely normal Albertans that are extremely happy with this legislation."[10]

This declaration of victory reminds me of another summary of parents' struggles, a rueful admission of defeat that came from a Pennsylvania pastor protesting the teaching of evolution, Ray Mummert. He said, "We're being attacked by the intelligent, educated segment of the culture."[11] Then he and his fellow concerned parents got into their gleaming vehicles and drove to their warm homes, where intelligence continued to assail them with light, medicine, clean tap water, and mod cons such as cable TV and the Internet.

As per the Paine principle, they're free to be walking contradictions, to believe in whatever blend of Jeebus and "I got mine, Jack" they like. Belief becomes a problem only when it encroaches on those institutions that people of diverse beliefs must share, when it leaks into the law or politics. Like when congregations in the South and the sticks and the suburbs aid and abet the installation of a Big Dad president who is the wonder-working tool of their Big Dad God.

The megachurches and pastorpreneurs that kept Republicans in office by urging their flocks to vote for them ought to pay reparations to sensible voters. Ditto for the Catholics and Mormons who stumped against gay marriage in states such as Maine and California. Yanking their tax-exempt status and slashing Christian corporate welfare would be a good start. It would send a very clear message that those who traduce the separation of Church and State must pay to play politics instead of profiteering from their unholy union. This brings us to . . .

Political freedom, or the end of authoritarian rule

I won't bang on at length about politics here, since I'll be doing that in Chapter Five. But I have to mention one of the most important legacies of the Enlightenment, the one we see in documents such as the American Declaration of Independence and the French Declaration of the Rights of Man and Citizen, which is the idea that liberty is a God-given or natural right. The only acceptable curb on this liberty is the liberty of others. As the French declaration states, "Liberty consists in the freedom to do everything which injures no one else; hence the exercise of the natural rights of each man has no limits except those which assure to the other members of the society the enjoyment of the same rights."

A king may be able to tamp down the violence and law-lessness and guarantee his subjects a modicum of security and commodious living, but he does so at the cost of the people's liberty and autonomy, a price that, by the end of the seventeenth century, enlightened people were no longer willing to pay. Locke, for example, argues that "absolute monarchy, which by some men is counted the only government in the world, is indeed inconsistent with civil society, and so can be no form of civil government at all."[12] Having a king means living under the rule of Big Dad.

If we are to have a rational polity, a democratic polity, then we must throw off the shackles of hereditary, arbitrary, traditional authority. Popping out of the lucky regal vagina is hardly a guarantee that the heir will know how to run things. Rather, the insular and privileged world of the aristocracy produces too many monarchs who are totally clueless about the concerns of the people. As Paine puts it in *Common Sense*,

> There is something exceedingly ridiculous in the composition of Monarchy: it first excludes a man from the means of information, yet empowers him to act in cases where the highest judgement is required. The state of a king shuts him from the World, yet the business of a king requires him to know it thoroughly.[13]

Fast forward to now. Are our democratic leaders shut from the World? Lord knows they press a lot of vulgar flesh, immersing themselves in ordinariness and hoping some of it will rub off, concealing such snobbish stains as an Ivy League education, a family fortune or, worse, brains – dangerous brains. But even though the campaign process and the business of governance mean meeting and mimicking the people, politicians still constitute an elite. To come within sniffing distance of public office, candidates require stacks of cash, bundles of donations. It's a sham to pretend otherwise, to keep staging this bumpkin burlesque and conducting elections as if everyone were running for Saltiest Salt of the Earth.

Conservative thinkers from Edmund Burke to Michael Oakeshott have cautioned that the Enlightenment demand for new laws instead of old traditions leads to utopianism, revolutionary violence, and the dissolution of established community bonds. You might start with a bunch of great ideas and do badass things like take over churches and rename the months of the year (Prairial, Messidor, Thermidor!), but it all ends in tumbrels and Terror.

The so-called conservatives who have been in and out of power since the eighties are actually revolutionaries in this pejorative sense. Your Reagans, Thatchers, and Bushes have created regimes that are far more radical and utopian than those of their liberal coevals. Their dogma – market fundamentalism – is not to be confused with fiscal conservatism or enlightened support of the free market as a freedom that fosters other freedoms. Which brings us to . . .

Economic freedom, or the liberation of trade
Conservatives and their compatriots in the business community complain that intellectuals are anti-capitalist. They allege that nerds are socialist moochers or simply inept, congenitally incapable of effectively monetizing their ideas. But this

ignores the stable of brains that the moneyed have bought and stored in a myriad of think tanks and foundations. These moneyed brains frequently plump for the Enlightenment in the same way that Glenn Beck flounces around in Founding Fathers drag. Regnery, one of the conservative movement's publishing houses, pushes eighteenth-century classics, such as Adam Smith's *Wealth of Nations* and *The Federalist Papers,* alongside its offerings from such contemporary *bien-pensants* as Michelle Malkin, Oliver North, and David Limbaugh, Rush's duller brother.

The thinkers of the Enlightenment did indeed have a generally favourable view of business and free trade. Brisk trade was one of the things that Voltaire admired about England. In a letter from his exile in London, he writes, "Commerce, which has enriched English citizens, has helped to make them free, and this freedom in its turn has extended commerce, and that has made the greatness of the nation."[14] Merchants were certainly preferable to lazy, corrupt aristocrats.

Voltaire also sang the praises of the London Stock Exchange, one of the few places in Europe where Jews and Muslims and all the fractious factions of Christendom did business freely and peaceably. At the Exchange, "a more respectable place than many a court . . . you will see the representatives of all nations gathered together for the utility of men."[15]

That bit about stock traders working for the utility of men might strike you as awfully quaint, but it's important to highlight it, because it is another aspect of our Enlightenment heritage that has fallen into disrepair. Now we call our traders masters of the universe, not servants of the people.

David Hume called merchants the "most useful" of men. But for Hume, industry, knowledge, and humanity were inextricably linked. He thought that

> [an] advantage of industry and of refinements in the mechanical arts is that they commonly produce some refinements in the liberal; nor can one be carried to perfection, without being accompanied, in some degree, with the other . . . We cannot reasonably expect, that a piece of woollen cloth will be wrought to perfection in a nation which is ignorant of astronomy, or where ethics are neglected.[16]

This holistic vision of the relation between commerce and culture is one of the most important of the Enlightenment's legacies, but it has been hijacked by market fundamentalists. They see commerce as an – arguably, the – end in itself. A piece of woollen cloth can be wrought by children or monkeys or robots for all they care, astronomy and ethics be damned.

The balance between culture and commerce is out of whack. We've lost sight of the thing that really is great about capitalism in our relentless pursuit of increased productivity and profit. We work ourselves into our graves, but Enlightenment thinkers embraced capitalism because increased efficiencies created more free time, which allowed people to pursue greater goals than merely subsisting and grovelling or getting and spending. Enlightenment thinkers were chuffed about the liberalization of trade and the first rumblings of the

Industrial Revolution because they were optimistic that hours once devoted to manual drudgery could now be spent figuring out clever new ways to cheat nature and God, to break the curse of unrelenting shitwork with further industrialization and technology. This would mean less and less drudgery and more time for tinkering with the things that really matter in life, such as poetry, classical philosophy, political polemics, amateur experiments, wine collecting, and the free exchange of ideas. Which brings us to . . .

Freedom of the pen, or public discourse and a rambunctious press

I won't linger on this topic too long either, as I will be looking at the press in detail in Chapter Six. But it is worth noting that the thinkers of the Enlightenment were fervent advocates of press freedom, and some, like those radical Frenchies Diderot and Voltaire, were martyred by censors and the police for writing smack about the Church and the aristocracy.

Here again we see that these Enlightenment freedoms are inseparable. Free inquiry, free votes, and free markets require public forums that allow us to exercise our reason. Free discourse and lively disputes, dissent, and debate are necessary if we are to pursue truth, be it in the form of a scientific experiment, a satirical poem, or a political system. This is why Kant argues that freedom of the pen is one of the most important freedoms. He says that "freedom of the pen is the only safeguard of the rights of the people." It also benefits the ruler, he argues, insofar as a ruler who stifles the opinions and complaints of the people "is thereby put into a self-stultifying position"[17]

England was the first country to allow a relatively free press, though one could still be prosecuted for libel and sedition. Enlightened despots such as Frederick II of Prussia also allowed more press freedom than their predecessors. The American Revolution was a pamphlet-fest, a flurry of polemics in partisan papers. And some states, such as Virginia and Massachusetts, already had clauses in their constitutions supporting freedom of the press.

There were bouts of backlash. Nevertheless, in spite of attempts to roll back press freedom, in Europe and North America the number of papers and publications, and the size of the literate public, grew by leaps and bounds throughout the eighteenth century. For example, the United Sates had only a handful of papers in the early 1700s, but more than three hundred by 1810.[18]

Now stories of the death of newspapers are ubiquitous, as everyone but the blue-hairs migrates from the antique broadsheet or tabloid to the electronic wilds of the Web, and papers die or cut entire departments such as book reviews or copy editing. Our press is suffering a slower, more ignoble demise than death by censorious tyrants. It is bleeding money and credibility, and its attempts to make more of the former mean liquidating more of the latter. The press tries to sell itself as an ally of the people, fighting for the common man, but polls show that the public does not believe this shtick. The media is not a forum for the free public exercise of reason, but simply another hated elite.

All four of these fields – religion, politics, markets, and the press – are rife with examples of the recrudescence of old authorities and traditions and a trivial sense of equality and liberty. The idea that your opinion, or my opinion, is just as good as anyone else's casts away evidence and reason, which play important roles in Enlightenment thought. The empirical bent that we see in many Enlightenment thinkers is an attempt to ground opinions and ideas on facts and observable phenomena that every rational sentient person has access to, instead of just saying "God says," "the King says," or "because it's always been this way."

The thinkers of the Enlightenment were guardedly optimistic about human potential, as they were quite skeptical about whether we could learn to think for ourselves and shuck off the pernicious influence of alien guidance. This is why education is so essential. Education helps us develop opinions based on evidence and to better evaluate others' opinions. It is also crucial in the development of common knowledge: a set of facts and standards we can all deploy in debates. This was the goal of one of the greatest Enlightenment projects, the French *Encyclopédie*. Diderot, the mastermind behind this project, said "All things must be examined, debated, investigated without exception and without regard to anyone's feelings."[19]

Is this the case today? Sadly, no. A goodly chunk of media-speak and political rhetoric exists for the express purpose of provoking feelings rather than reasonable arguments about the facts. Then there are the forbidden facts, concealed in the interest of national and corporate security. Any number of examinations, debates, and investigations can never bubble up to the level of public attention lest they adversely affect some industry, leak strategically valuable information, spark litigation, or transgress one of our new articles of faith. And one of those new articles of faith, conveniently enough, is that we are the freest people in the world.

I saw an ad on TV not long ago that began and ended with the declaration "Free expression is what I'm all about," a sentiment sure to meet with near-universal approval. But the product the ad was pushing was Botox, a poison that freezes your face into a stiff rictus that creepily approximates youth. Again – and in the most literal way – we see immaturity and consumption marketed as freedom.

It isn't just that we are frittering away our freedom by succumbing to the parental charms of dogma and backsliding into alien guidance. North Americans have also chosen and created some really shitty, insipid dogmas. Hectoring demagogues run the gamut from ham-fisted literalist Christians and talk-radio yapflappers and marketeering mammonists to paranoiac 9/11 conspiracy theorists and condescending vegans. There is also the healthism that every gym and diet product and lifestyle pill consecrates, that every smoking ban and anti-trans-fat law enshrines, a nannying that thrives cheek by jowl with rampant unhealth and obesity. And then there's the less sweaty version of this me-centricity and its twee New Age variants: the self-helpist narcissism that keeps the publishing industry alive.

The freedom that North American leaders extol is largely content-free, and duty-free too. Once in a while we have to pretend to remember the soldiers who died for it back in the day and send warm fuzzies to the ones dying for it now. Other than that, freedom-speak is a whole lotta "you can be whatever you want to be" hogwash, punctuated by orders to shop and to work.

We are not adults in the sense that Kant intended, but adolescents. This is a problem, because we are also the world's most heavily armed teenagers. We have relentlessly extended the bounds of technical reason to the point that it has supplanted humane reason – the kind of thinking you find in history, literature, and philosophy. The problem is that technical reason is not Thought 2.0, an upgrade that replaces the buggy betas of ethics and history. Technical reason cannot replace humane reason. Rather, it demands great lashings of it. Comedian Patton Oswalt has a hilarious routine about a sixty-seven-year-old woman giving birth. At one point in his rant, he says that science is "all about the coulda, not the shoulda."[20] He's right. We've augmented our coulda powers in fantastic ways, but our capacity for thinking about the shoulda has shrivelled. Enter Glenn Beck and Dr. Phil to fill the void.

Jefferson was adamant that an educated populace was necessary to maintain the republic, and he wrote about the need for public schools where everyone could learn to read, write, reason, do math, and study history, as these were the basic skills required for self-governance. Without education and general knowledge, the people were all too susceptible to flattery, fear-mongering, and demagoguery. In one of his many letters on this topic, he anticipates the bumper-sticker chestnut "If you think education is expensive, try ignorance."

> Preach, my dear Sir, a crusade against ignorance; establish and improve the law for educating the common people. Let our countrymen know that the people alone can protect us against these evils, and that the tax which will be paid for this purpose is not more than the thousandth part of what will be paid to kings, priests and nobles who will rise up among us if we leave the people in ignorance.[21]

In his final years, Jefferson made his ideas about education concrete, founding and designing the University of Virginia. It was one of the first schools in America to offer a political science program, and it had no faculty of theology or a campus chapel. Instead, the centre of Jefferson's campus was the library, housed in a rotunda he modelled on the Parthenon.

It's very picturesque and makes for a great photo op. Perhaps this is why, way back in 1989, when Bush the Elder called a meeting of the fifty U.S. governors to discuss national standards for the education system, they met at the University of Virginia. It may be difficult to remember this two decades later, after watching his son play the role of edjumacation prezdint, but Bush the First also pitched himself as an education president. Speaking from the steps of the Rotunda, he called for national performance indicators for schools and urged "tradition-shattering reform." First on the agenda? "I see the day when every student is literate," quoth Poppy, shooting for the stars.

I have to give the man points for insisting that America must be a "reading nation," even though he wrapped this fine principle in the usual blah-dee-blah about staying competitive in the international market. He omitted the salutary effects of reading that Jefferson endorsed, such as not becoming – or voting for – complete fuckwits, but he did ask the following excellent question:

> Education is our most enduring legacy, vital to everything we are and can become. And come the next century – just ten years away – what will we be? Will we be children of the Enlightenment or its orphans?[22]

More than a decade later, in 2000, his son posed a similar question: "Rarely is the question asked: is our children learning?" The difference between these two quotes says a lot, and none of it good. Even the president's childrens is not learning. Is this because our schools is sucking?

Chapter Three

IS OUR SCHOOLS SUCKING?

*And liberty cannot be preserved without a general knowledge
among the people, who have a right, from the frame of their
nature, to knowledge, as their great Creator, who does nothing
in vain, has given them understandings, and a desire to know . . .
the preservation of the means of knowledge among the lowest
ranks, is of more importance to the public than all the property
of all the rich men in the country.*

— JOHN ADAMS[1]

E ven though the school systems in the U.S. and Canada
are governed by a patchwork of state and provincial
regulations, schools sucking has become a trusty
political football all over North America. Education is a campaign stump staple and a perpetual crisis, one many crusaders can cut to fit their cause. Fundies, lefties, righties, and
customarily apolitical people worried about their wee ones all
spin the state of the schools to support their opposing pet
initiatives. They can advance their particular agenda, be it
religious, political, environmental, or purely selfish, in the

name of the children, thus racking up double concern points. Triple, if you equate children and the future. Recycling/Jesus + Babies + All Our Tomorrows = Very Important Issue/ Person indeed.

For politicians, education is a reliable source of photo ops and flights of rhetoric, as it gives them a valuable opportunity to wax enthusiastic about children and the future – two things they have yet to fuck up. You know the drill: mouth some well-meaning mush about how much math and science and reading rilly, rilly matter in the twenty-first century, tousle some moppet's hair, feign interest in the classroom tchotchkes, finagle some mom-and-pop votes.

They can also use the state of the schools to go dire and forecast doom. This sort of school panic-speak is a watered-down long-range version of the politics of fear that has prevailed since 9/11. If immediate perils such as terrorists, a rising China, or wussification by Eurosocialism do not destroy North America first, someday all our stupid children will. Our failed schools will render them too stunned and broke to run the machines and dole out the meds we expect to ease us through our dotage. And our children's children will be utterly barbaric and bereft, wandering some blasted Mad Max hellscape, barely able to recall the recipe for fire, even though everything around them is burning, endlessly burning.

School crisis stories are a manifestation of our worries about the future and our widespread concern about the children. But they are also one of the ways we express our anxiety about our collective intelligence. "Is our children learning?" is another way of asking, "Is us getting dumber?" If we are, what chance do we have of remaining competitive in the global market, keeping up with countries that seem to have better school systems, students, and adult literacy rates than we do? Mediocre to crappy student test scores are one of the signs that we may soon end up the bitches of those diligent high-scoring Asians, Indians, and Scandinavians, unless everyone works harder, faster, better, smarter, more.

Schools are also a staging ground in the culture wars that have waxed and waned since the eighties. But righty and lefty criticisms of the school system are more similar than they initially appear, thanks to their common adherence to some of the anti-nerd notions I discussed in the first chapter. The right claims that schools are socialist indoctrination centres where their lil' spuds get soaked in government and gaydom. The left claims that the schools are corporate brainwashing facilities that teach kids to be obedient little office drones, stunting their creativity and curiosity, plying them with junk food and ads and pointless busywork. They may blame different causes – well, slightly different, given the tender intimacy betwixt government and business – but they level similar charges, arguing that education is nothing more than propaganda or brainwash.

The propaganda campaign that passes for education is one of the ways those dastardly nerds exert their control over society as a whole, by wrecking kids, setting up camp in their dear little heads when they are young and vulnerable. Schools change tiny minds. The implication on both sides is that they should not. Go far enough to the left or the right or towards some god, and you will find ardent parents' rights advocates who think – no, *know* – that they know better than their children's teachers.

North America's decentralized school systems are perfect conveyances for passing the smelly blame, ensuring that there will be way more speeches than solutions. Parents can blame lazy teachers. Teachers can blame lazy parents. Teachers can blame administrators. Administrators can blame the school boards. School boards can blame their cheapskate, tax-averse districts or their greedy unionized employees. Or they can pass the blame along to the state and provincial educrats, who then blame the feds for providing insufficient funds. The feds plead poverty and blame everything from *Grand Theft Auto* to teachers' unions to bureaucratic waste for the situation, tap dancing as they try not to alienate the voluminous voting blocs of concerned parents and unions.

But are our schools really sucking? This turns out to be one of those issues where people hate the species and the system but approve of the examples they know – a "lawyers are assholes but mine is fine" thing. For forty years Phi Beta Kappa has commissioned a yearly Gallup poll of Americans' attitudes towards public schools, and they've found that "the closer the public gets to its local schools, the more it likes them."[2]

Parents consistently give big, broad categories such as "the national schools" and "the schools in my community" middling to bad grades, and they say that schools in Europe and Asia are better. But they also tend to be positive about local schools: the ones their children attend. In 2008, 72 per cent of respondents gave their kid's school a grade of A or B. This is the most positive rating that public schools have received in fifteen years. To grade the grade, three-quarters represents a C-plus or B-minus, but that result is still much better than the speeches, coverage, and op eds lead us to believe.

The school crisis rhetoric is milder up north, but the grades are comparable. One poll, conducted by the Canadian Education Association in 2007, found that 42 per cent of the respondents gave the schools B's, and 33 per cent a gentleman's C.[3] A 2008 CBC poll had similar results. Only 8 per cent said that the schools were excellent, but 49 per cent, an overwhelming majority, said they were good, and 28 per cent thought they were adequate. Moreover, the number of parents who gave schools the lowest possible ratings – poor and very poor – decreased substantially from the 1990s, dropping from 25 per cent to 14 per cent.[4]

Asking parents how much they like their kids' schools is only one measure of the school system, though. Schools do not merely serve parents, and sometimes parental needs and public needs clash. For example, some parents might gripe about social promotion and every student getting gold stars, only to quickly change their tune when their son or daughter flunks. Easy A's might look great stuck on the family fridge, but they don't help create a competent workforce, informed citizenry, or civil society.

Other measures of school performance are less encouraging. Millions of North American high-school graduates are functionally illiterate and innumerate, and woefully ignorant of basic history and science. The collegiate *crème de la crème* that I see are literate-ish at best. Some can be quite intellectually timid and unwilling to think for themselves.

The passivity, nervousness, and heartbreaking inarticulacy of some of my students is evidence that the school system is not doing a super job teaching kids to read, write, and think. Sometimes I read work by students whose grammar is practically feral – utterly untutored. They claim their teachers never taught them about the niceties of sentence structure; instead they did quizzes and got to watch movies in English class. Students can pass English without the fuss and bother of comprehending its basic concepts, and I have no reason to believe that things are any better in the math, science, or history departments. This suggests that some of the worries about schools may well be justified.

At the same time, though, a lot of the crisis-in-the-schools rhetoric comes from some bad political ideas, ideas that have been setting the tone for public policy and discourse for more than twenty years, ideas that are partly responsible for the mess we're in now. Decrying the evil socialist gub'mint monopoly on schools is an example of the demonization of all things public. Anti-school rants quickly slide into anti-union ranting, since "unions R bad" is another one of our modern, plutocrat-friendly articles of faith.

This is one of the reasons why charter schools are oft mentioned in debates about the state of the schools. Conservatives favour charter schools because they offer an end run around the teachers' unions, more scope for hiring, firing, and unpaid overtime, and greater curricular freedom. But there are very lefty charter schools too, ones that focus on environmental education, the arts, or social justice. Charters also have powerful allies in the political centre. The Obama administration has promised increased funding for charter schools as part of its $4.35 billion Race to the Top program, one of the education components of the stimulus package.

Charter schools are a relatively new idea. They exist somewhere in between public and private schools, as they are publicly funded but privately run. The first state to pass a law allowing charters was Minnesota, in 1991. By 2009, according to the Center for Education Reform, a pro-charter group, 4,578 charter schools were operating in the U.S., schooling approximately 1.4 million K–12 students.[5] In Canada, Alberta was the first province to allow charter schools, in 1994, and now has thirteen. No other Canadian province has followed suit yet, though Quebec, British Columbia, and Torontonia have for decades offered partial public funding to independent alternative schools.

Those who support charter schools argue that they provide parents with more choices and that market competition will stimulate somnolent public schools. Allowing all manner of specialized schools, from the strictly religious to the just plain strict to the environmentally pious, further decentralizes the school system and cedes more control to local, parental, and private interests. This is precisely what school-choice advocates seek. To give just one cartoony example, John Stossel, in a 2006 ABC news special called "Stupid in America," made a strong case for vouchers and charters as market solutions to the corrupt state monopoly on education. He said that a state-run school was as silly as a state-run grocery store. Without the prod of competition, your gub'mint grocer would doubtless peddle overpriced bread and curdled milk. Ditto for the sucky socialist schools, which had made American children stupider than Belgians.

Stossel was pop-eyed with outrage. *Belgians were free to choose their schools. Their kids were smarter.* Chocolate-confecting, mussel-slurping semi-French Euroweenies were enjoying more choices than the future citizens of the freest, best country on earth? *Quelle horreur!*

While it is true that Belgians have a voucher system in which the funds follow the students, they also have a national curriculum and national standards, so it isn't quite a market free-for-all like the riot of chip flavours in the snack aisle. Moreover, Belgians also have other educational policies, such as free early childhood education, that help account for their edge on international tests. The Belgian system, like many European systems, practises streaming, separating the vocationally inclined and the college-bound much earlier than Canadian and American schools do. Can you imagine the howls of indignation from self-proclaimed libertarians like Stossel if American educrats were exerting such sway over children's career paths?

Streaming and state-subsidized early childhood education are European in the bad way. They represent socialist interventions in family life, encroachments of the nanny state at its nanniest. School choice, conversely, is all about the power of markets. Defenders of school choice praise the market's ability to satisfy proliferating particular niches. It is also about parent power, the firm conviction that Stossel's audience – or severely normal Albertans or devout Christian, Jewish, and Muslim parents – know what is best for their children.

Don't get me wrong. I think parents certainly have the right to raise their children as they see fit, and that they love their children more than anyone else. But love does not qualify someone to explain cell division, long division, or the War of 1812. School-choice rhetoric is another case of feelings, such as parental love, trumping the nerdy expertise of the people who actually run the schools and teach the kids. Moreover, parental rights issues get legally murky when parents suckle their kids on beliefs that make them social pariahs, like the White Pride mom in Winnipeg who drew swastikas on her kid before sending her off to school – repeatedly.

Maybe this unpleasantness could have been avoided if only there were a neo-Nazi charter school to meet her child's unique educational needs. Studying the Second World War in a mainstream history class could be a real blow to the self-esteem of a kid raised as a fake Aryan. At the Stormfront Skool of Traditional Values (home of the Fighting Hitlers), the poor child would be spared the trauma of having her culture and her family's choices disrespected.

This is, admittedly, an exaggerated example of the school market's vast potential for diversification. But it does help illustrate that school-choice-speak is often another form of anti-intellectualism, a rejection of the educational establishment and professional nerds. Charter schools are appealing because they suggest that almost anyone can open a school and run it more cheaply and cheerfully than the hidebound old bureaucracies can. They imply that the solutions to problems in the schools are really simple and that educrats suffer from elitist delusions of complexity. Charter schools also appeal to our preference for action, as opposed to thought. They insinuate that education profs who produce studies about charter schools are constructing castles of theory but the entrepreneurs who open charter schools are doing something that makes a difference.

Critics of charter schools contend that the school-choice movement is just a sneaky way of permitting increased privatization and bypassing teachers' unions. Allowing a market of specialized schools to bloom on the public dime also undermines one of the missions of public schools: the idea that public schools are common schools, social glue, institutions that provide a set of shared reference points and skills, a sense of culture and history, and basic scientific and mathematical knowledge.

Another common argument against charters is that they shred the commonality of the school system in another way, by cherry-picking the best students and most concerned parents from communities and dumping special needs and high-risk kids back into the public system. Some jurisdictions have even made charter schools admit students via lotteries, to prevent them from skimming the student and parental cream from every district. But that doesn't entirely dispel the selection bias here, as the parents who apply for the lotto are obviously more motivated than the ones who do not.

The jury is still out on whether charter schools perform better than their public counterparts. Advocates claim that they do, but a recent study, released by Stanford University in 2009, found that only 17 per cent of charter schools were performing better than their public counterparts. More than a third – 37 per cent – fared worse than public schools, and 46 per cent did not differ in any significant way, for better or for worse.[6]

As the Stanford researchers note, one of the problems with rating charter-school performance is that there are many kinds, with different missions, subject to varying state and provincial requirements. And even when they do work as schools, it remains to be seen whether charters can work as businesses. Several charter schools have collapsed because of fiscal mismanagement. A 2009 study conducted in Minnesota found that only 24 of the state's 145 charter schools had clean books; the other 121 had some fiscal irregularities.[7]

The most high-profile example of charter schools failing to fulfil their promise of improved efficiency is the chain formerly known as Edison Schools Inc. The Edison chain, much hyped in the 1990s, was the brainchild of businessman and edupreneur Chris Whittle. You can also thank Whittle for Channel One, the network he started in 1989, which loaned schools AV equipment in exchange for broadcasting its infoadvertainment in classrooms. Whittle sold Channel One in 1994 in the midst of a blaze of bad publicity about his tax and accounting snafus.

Still, the media, particularly right-wing organs such as the *Wall Street Journal*, hailed Edison Schools as a revolution, a sleek new for-profit model of education. But the company consistently hemorrhaged cash, was investigated by the Securities and Exchange Commission for filing inaccurate financial statements, and had some of its contracts cancelled by local boards. The company has since rebranded itself as EdisonLearning Inc., a source of educational software. Edison still manages schools in twenty-four states, but it reverted to private company status in 2003 after the chain's stock price plummeted. Ironically, its fiscal saviours included the very public school teachers that Edison was competing against – the Florida State Employees Pension Fund bought the company.

The current charter-school media darling is the Knowledge Is Power Program, a.k.a. KIPP schools. Created in 1994 by two alums from the newbie-teacher mission Teach for America, KIPP schools serve poor inner-city communities. The majority of their students are black or Latino, and parents must sign contracts that obligate them to take an active role in their child's education. KIPP students spend longer hours in the classroom than their public-school counterparts. The school day starts earlier and ends later, and there are Saturday and summer sessions at most schools too.

Some KIPP schools have shown good results, but critics of the program argue that these gains depend on a pool of young, idealistic teachers willing to put in long hours for low pay. KIPP teachers in some New York City schools have even started to unionize, much to the chagrin of the anti-union wing of the charter-school booster club. I don't condone making teachers work ill- or unpaid overtime, something that many instructors, publicly or privately managed, already do. However, I do like the KIPPsters' extended school hours; the public-school day and year should be longer.

Very few North American children spend their summers helping with the harvest. The current school year is a silly agrarian anachronism, one that leaves working parents scrambling for child-care options. But I suspect I may be in the minority here, and that many taxpayers, teachers' unions, parents, and kids would object to way more school, for both fiscal and personal reasons.

The other noteworthy aspect of the KIPP program is its focus on getting poor kids into college. Even though most KIPP schools are middle schools (junior highs), students are encouraged to think of themselves as college material and bust their butts accordingly. It's laudable that KIPP schools are helping more poor and minority students make it to university, where they are still underrepresented. But broad school reforms cannot take the KIPP approach and steer everyone towards university. We need skilled tradespeople and college-trained professionals too. Public schools, particularly those in affluent school districts, already act as if university is for everybody, even though they do a half-assed job of making sure everybody is ready for university.

Despite my commitment to the battered and venerable public education system, I must concede that public schools are not great at preparing kids for college. Colleges and universities in North America offer thousands of remedial classes so their students can acquire the basic math and English skills they really should have learned many grades before. A 2006 survey of high-school teachers and college profs conducted by the *Chronicle of Higher Education* shows a major difference of opinion between high-school teachers and the professoriate with respect to student preparation for college. A full 44 per cent of the profs thought students were ill-prepared for the rigours of college writing, while 36 per cent of the high-school teachers thought their former charges were well-prepared to write at the college level. A measly 6 per cent of the profs concurred with that rosy assessment of their students' word power. The same was true for math, with 37 per cent of the high-school teachers thinking that students were well-prepared for college math, but only 2 per cent of profs agreeing.[8]

I do not buy the catastrophic rhetoric about schools, as so much of it comes from politically suspect sources. But public schools could and should be doing a much better job teaching kids to think, read, and write. I've seen the results of both education systems, in classrooms on either side of the border, and some are pretty glum, chum.

I've had a couple of students brag that they made it through the school system and into college without ever reading an entire book. Several of my students have wigged out about writing essays, claiming that none of their other teachers ever made such unreasonable demands. Couldn't I just tell them what the poems and novels meant, and then test them? That's how they learned to learn in regular school. Their K–12 teachers were kindly mama birds, willing to chew up the worms and spit the goopy food into their eager beaks.

There's nothing like teaching quasi-adults basic argumentation and the rudiments of grammar to make one wonder what the hell they – and their teachers – have been doing for the past twelve years. Apparently I am not alone. Wondering what and how teachers are doing has become public policy, in the form of increased, and increasingly important, standardized testing programs. In January 2002 President Bush signed the No Child Left Behind Act, the most sweeping federal reform of the education system in years. The principal provision of NCLB was yearly high-stakes testing in English and math.

Standardized tests are another manifestation of our obsession with quantifying – reducing everything to metrics and scores and discounting anything that cannot be converted into numbers. The standardized testing industry has grown into a multi-billion-dollar business, thanks to pols and taxpayers spazzing out about accountability and transparency, demanding to know exactly how much brain-bang they're getting for their tax bucks. Fairtest, an advocacy organization devoted to test reform, estimates that American schools administer a hundred million standardized tests a year.[9]

The Heritage Foundation, an uber-conservative think tank, has argued that NCLB "increased state and local governments' annual paperwork burden by 6,680,334 hours, at an estimated cost of $141 million."[10] And over on the other side of the aisle, some argue that this tide of paperwork is unreliable at best. A report by the think tank Education Sector, called "The Pangloss Index: How States Game the No Child Left Behind Act," criticizes the Enronesque digit-juggling that educators use to claim their schools are always improving, just as Voltaire's Pangloss claimed that we live in the best of all possible worlds.

The report uses the embattled Birmingham, Alabama, school district as its exemplary case, detailing the way state and local officials played with numbers and sample sizes to produce the illusion of astounding improvements. Other states, such as Missouri, met test goals by lowering standards for proficiency. Then there were loophole-hunting trailblazers such as Tennessee's educrats, who came up with the following end run around those tough new rules:

> Districts would only be identified as "in need of improvement" if they missed the state performance target in *all three grade spans* – elementary, middle, and high school – in the same subject, for two consecutive years. A district could fail two-thirds of its students every year and never be held accountable, as long as it wasn't exactly the *same* two-thirds.[11]

This tactic was a big hit; twenty-eight other states got permission from the Department of Education to do their numbers this way too.

Another problem with test-heavy schemes like NCLB is that they provide openings for privatization by stealth. In a 2008 interview with *Time* magazine, Susan Neuman, a former Department of Education official, conceded that a number of her ex-colleagues "saw the NCLB as a Trojan horse for the choice agenda – a way to expose the failure of public education and 'blow it up a bit . . . There were a number of people pushing hard for market forces and privatization.'"[12] This is in keeping with the market-fundamentalist creed that private industry does everything better than public services, which assumes that profit-making entities and public services exist for the same reasons and should operate the same way. Do you really want your child's education to be *efficient?* I seriously doubt that is the first adjective that leaps to mind.

Even if you accept the criterion of efficiency, public/ private educational initiatives often fail by their own standards. Let me give you an example from my own backyard, as a cautionary tale for other school districts. In the 1990s, Nova Scotia needed to build dozens of new schools. The Liberal government entered into public/private partnerships ("P3s") in 1994, signing contracts to build fifty-five new schools. The provincial auditor estimated that the P3 schools boondoggle ended up costing $32 million more than building the schools by tender as usual, thanks to cost overruns, construction delays, and expensive arbitration sessions to determine which P was responsible for various costs and liabilities.

Critics alleged that the point of the P3 arrangement was not to save money but to make it look like we were, by keeping school debts off the books. By the year 2000 the program had to be totally scrapped, but Nova Scotia taxpayers are still paying for it, and will be for quite some time, as many of the P3 schools are being leased back to the government for years to come. And the private contractors pulled all sorts of classy moves that tell you a lot about their interest in and commitment to such partnerships, like trying to claw back vending-machine revenue and cash from the sale of chocolate bars by students, and charging usurious fees to school teams and community groups using school spaces.

It's bad enough that kids have to peddle overpriced candy to pay for their extracurricular activities. But for chisellers to be standing by, ready to snatch the chump change from their tiny hands lest it be wasted on luxuries such as band and basketball? This Grinchy conduct makes me doubt that privatization is a panacea. Instead it seems to be an invitation for pseudo-capitalist leeches to profiteer at the community's expense.

The other problem with standardized testing programs like NCLB is the idea that learning can be inventoried like cheap Chinese toys in a Wal-Mart warehouse. Speaking at a Washington charter school in 2006, Dubya said:

> Oh, I know people say we test too much, but how can you solve a problem until you measure? And how can you hold people to account when there's an achievement gap that is not right for America, unless you measure? Measuring is the gateway to success.[13]

First, it's not like we need more tests to show us the glaringly obvious achievement gaps. Innumerable studies demonstrate that students who are poor do worse than middle-class or affluent students. Second, the idea of accountability that Bush peddled presumes that teachers, school boards, and education experts should answer to the tight-fisted taxpayers who pay their salaries, a perfect example of the more-money-than-brains mindset at work.

There is nothing inherently good about measures, as any red-blooded American opponent of the devil's own metric system can attest. In a speech protesting the U.K.'s batteries of standardized tests, British teacher Robert Palmer said the following, which I cannot improve upon:

> Our education system is now strangled by the dead hand of Gradgrindism. Is this it, then? Is this all education is about, a series of hoops to jump through? Is this why we became teachers, so we could teach to the test, hold the hoops for our pupils just a little bit higher every time?[14]

Gradgrindism is a nice neologism. Palmer is referring to Thomas Gradgrind, the relentlessly utilitarian headmaster from Dickens's *Hard Times.* Dickens lampooned Gradgrind's nothing-but-the-facts approach to education, using the headmaster as a symbol of the heartless calculation of the Industrial Revolution – the same calculating mindset that still drives standardized testing policies.

Let me be perfectly clear. I'm not some hippie who thinks that rote learning has no place in education. Hell, no. Students definitely require a body of *who, where, what, when,* and *why* in order to ascend to higher-order thinking. The problem with test-o-centric policies is that they stop where a real education begins, at the level of scattered facts and basic skills.

Maybe the boomers and fogies who pitch these testing policies haven't taken enough of the damn things to understand how students react to them. Most standardized tests are just multiple-choice fill-in-the-bubble forms. I remember taking the provincial versions as a kid every couple of years. We all knew that they didn't really affect our grades, so wiseacres would invariably pencil in the bubbles to form dirty doodles or repeatedly spell AC/DC. We didn't care, because the tests didn't count. Now, given that funding and staffing decisions ride on those little graphite-filled bubbles, the tests matter. It is education in the broad sense that does not count anymore, that must be shoved aside so kids can cram for multiple-choice quizzes.

I object to the Gradgrindist bias that determines much of the available research on education. Policy analysts and think tanks could and should write about schools in a more substantive, qualitative way rather than relying on numbers and rankings, treating schools as *Consumer Reports* covers cars. But numbers are the coin of the realm in a more-money-than-brains world, so numbers are what we get. And then opposing camps such as teachers' unions and corporate lobbyists spin the same stats to declare the same school systems the world's finest or total failures.

How dire are the North American numbers, relative to the rest of the globe? Let's start with one test, the Programme for International Student Assessment (PISA), the OECD's triennial survey of the aptitudes of fifteen-year-olds from many lands. In 2006 they tested teens' science powers. Canadian students placed third, behind Finland and China/Hong Kong. The U.S scored eleven points below the 500-point average, placing twenty-ninth on the OECD scale, right between scientific powerhouses Latvia and the Slovak Republic. Its math skills, the main focus of the 2003 PISA study, were also below average. American students got 474, two points less than Azerbaijan, but seven points more than the next country on the list, Croatia. Hong Kong and Finland led the pack, with scores in the upper 540s, while Canadian students ranked third, scoring in the 530s.[15]

Another set of international rankings, the Progress in International Reading Literacy Study, which assesses fourth-graders, also rated U.S. performance as middle of the pack. In the glass-half-full argot favoured by America's National Center for Education Statistics, 2006 scores were "higher than the average score of students in 22 of the 44 other countries and educational jurisdictions that participated in the PIRLS assessment."[16] Some of the jurisdictions that outperformed the U.S. include the Canadian provinces that participate in the PIRLS, Luxembourg, Singapore, Russia, and Latvia.

The United States does win the bronze medal in one OECD scholastic performance indicator: spending. Only Israel and Iceland spend a greater percentage of their GDP on educational institutions than Americans do. The next trio of countries on the spend-a-lot list are Korea, Denmark, and New Zealand. Some of them have better results to show for their spending: Korea's and New Zealand's scores are above average. But some of them do not, which just goes to show that funding isn't the only factor that determines educational success.

Another thing worth noting about these figures is that Korea and the U.S. both spend a lot of private money on education. The rate of funding for U.S. public schools is actually below the OECD average, but the heaps of cash spent on private tuition at schools and colleges drives the overall average up. Moreover, this sort of survey doesn't keep track of all the money people spend on child-improving para-educational whatnot, a bustling business that starts with Lamaze toys and Baby Einstein videos and continues through extracurricular activities and lessons and test prep programs, summer camps, and educational video games.

Nevertheless, despite all the spondulicks and speeches devoted to education, the high-school dropout rate in America has risen. Back in the 1960s, the U.S. led the world in high-school completion, but in 2005 they placed twenty-first out of the twenty-seven OECD countries surveyed. The census data for 2007 says that 86 per cent of Americans twenty-five or older have at least completed high school, a figure that includes GED (General Equivalency/Educational Diploma) holders. But some economists have found this number suspiciously rosy.

One study, done in 2008 by economists James Heckman and Paul LaFontaine, says that inclusion of the GED inflates the numbers. GED holders, who log less class time and test their way to a diploma, do about as well in the workplace as dropouts do. Their projections are not nearly as optimistic as the official numbers. They insist that

> (1) the U.S. high school graduation rate peaked at around 80 per cent in the late 1960s and then declined by 4–5 percentage points; (2) the actual high school graduation rate is substantially lower than the 88 per cent estimate; (3) about 65 percent of blacks and Hispanics leave school with a high school diploma, and minority graduation rates

are still substantially below the rates for non-
Hispanic whites.[17]

In 2008, when the California school system got a long-
awaited student-tracking system up and running, they found
that one-quarter of their students dropped out. This was an
improvement over some estimates, but much worse than the
previous official numbers.[18]

The experts may still be squabbling about the data, but
one thing is clear. Dropping out of high school makes it way
more likely that one will end up in the slammer, on social
assistance, or in the worn-to-a-frazzle ranks of the working
poor.

The Canadian dropout rate has been decreasing steadily
since the 1990s. According to Statistics Canada, it fell from 16.6
per cent in 1990–91 to 9.3 per cent in 2006–07. The majority of
dropouts, in both Canada and the U.S., are young men. In
Canada the problem is more rural than urban, with the highest
dropout rates occurring in Quebec and the prairie provinces.

It's worth noting that Alberta's dropout rate is above the
national average, which helps to explain why Alberta schools
score well in international assessments. The easy availability
of oil-patch gigs lures most of the uninterested, low-scoring
types out of the system, making Alberta experiments such
as charter schools look more successful than they might be.
Conversely, the east coast made the greatest gains in high-
school completion. This makes sense, as the primary and
secondary industries that used to pull young men out of
classrooms and into lucrative labour – the fisheries and plants

that used to be our oil sands – have gone belly-up, so more people are staying in school.

The United States is split about the value of education. There's a lot of hullabaloo about the state of the schools, but there is also more respect for unschooled, self-made successes. It has become an article of faith in Canada that people need education to succeed, which is one of the reasons why our public-school squabbles are not nearly so heated as those of our southern neighbours.

Canadian students tend to do well in international tests. In the PISA math and reading test results released in 2006, Canadian students performed above the OECD averages, placing seventh in math and fourth in reading. I'm not mentioning this so I can enjoy a gloating Canuck moment. Americans have a national education department and a national dialogue about the issue, which is more than I can say for my boring homeland. Sure, that conversation includes a lot of hysteria and crazy talk, but Canadians have no federal education portfolio or much in the way of a national conversation about schools.

Stephen Harper and his Cons are unlikely to start one. There's barely a word about education in the party's platform or on their policy website. Whenever Cons talk about education, they really mean trraining, a mere means to some job. And when Cons broach the topic of young people, they are usually talking about sending them to jail or to Afghanistan, not college or university. Inmates and soldiers, cons and cops, wardens and warriors – unlike lazy teachers and slack students – never get the whole summer off.

The gap between Canadian and U.S. test scores is interesting because it helps us rule out one of the usual excuses for poor student performance. Little Canucklings have equal access to all the distractions that cultural conservatives and pandering candidates blame for the stupefaction of youth. Canadian kids eat the same lousy food, watch the same moronic reality TV, play the same shoot-'em-up video games, and listen to the same dippy party rap as their southern coevals.

It is way too easy to blame *Grand Theft Auto* and text messaging for poor student performance. Sure, some pop culture glorifies anti-intellectualism, but the gap between Canadian and American test scores – and the fact that crabapples once said the exact same things about comic books, jazz, and the talkies – show us that pop culture is not really the problem.

The most important factor in determining student performance is class. Poor students do poorly: a class divide that ensures future class divisions, undermining the meritocratic North American dream, the idea that poor people can, by dint of their hard work and smarts, do better than their forebears did. This ideal still brings immigrants to our fair shores, and in Canada, the children of immigrants are much more likely to complete high school and finish university degrees.

The term *meritocracy* is fairly new, coined in 1958 by British sociologist and politico Michael Young. Young was quite dismayed by popular adoption of the term, since he meant it pejoratively. *The Rise of the Meritocracy* was a dystopian satire of the new elite. Young worried that the education system was rewarding a narrow set of skills, such as doing well on IQ tests or getting into the right brand-name schools. The meritocracy, Young argues, is just as unequal as the traditional British class structure, and even more disingenuous for pretending that anyone can succeed and that success is proof of merit. The poorly educated and just plain poor become embittered and disenfranchised, and the successes become smug at best and hubristic at worst.

In a 2001 editorial for *The Guardian*, Young wrote:

> The business meritocracy is in vogue. If meritocrats believe, as more and more of them are encouraged to, that their advancement comes from their own merits, they can feel they deserve whatever they can get. They can be insufferably smug, much more so than . . . the beneficiaries of nepotism. The newcomers can actually believe they have morality on their side. So assured have the elite become that there is almost no block on the rewards they arrogate to themselves.[19]

This is a pretty prescient description of the rhetoric we've heard lately from the geniuses of Wall and Bay streets. The successful routinely invoke the meritocratic bona fides of a system that tells them they are meritorious.

Still, North Americans exhibit a positively romantic attachment to the notion that Canada and the U.S are indeed meritocracies, societies that reward smarts and hard work. Meritocracy is an important part of Barack and Michelle Obama's appeal; both frequently stress that they are poor scholarship students who have made good. People long for examples of meritocracy in action because they are worried that their cherished dreams will not come true. Politics, pop culture, and self-help all sell assurances that we will succeed, but the demand for such assurances shows that we are really anxious about our prospects.

A 2008 Zogby poll on attitudes in the American workplace found that three-quarters of U.S. workers thought the American dream was less attainable than it had been eight years earlier. Another study on economic mobility, conducted by the Pew Charitable Trusts in concert with lefty and righty think tanks, found that the American dream was alive and well – in Canada, France, and the Scandinavian countries, where citizens were twice as economically mobile as people in the United States or the United Kingdom.[20]

You may recall from a few short pages ago that countries such as Canada and the Scandinavian nations scored better than the U.S. on international tests. Coincidence? I think not. More economic mobility means more resources at home and more incentive to do well. Less economic mobility means more fatalism and resignation on the part of poor students and more dreams of winning the class lotto the way people on TV and in movies do, through luck and pluck and looks and the kinds of talents one develops over the course of an inspirational montage.

In the United States, the middle class has been more rudely and vigorously screwed by its financial betters than it has in Canada, so it stands to reason that Canuck schools score better on average and that U.S. schools exhibit greater extremes. America has some of the world's most highly respected schools, but they exist a world away from the under-funded, overcrowded ones that serve the students who most desperately need a good education. Even Dubya knew this was the big problem. Programs such as KIPP and Teach for America have made laudable efforts to improve impover-ished schools. Some American school districts have also real-ized that class affects the classroom, and they are opting to modify their race-based integration policies to class-plus-race formulas.

But this isn't just a question of cash; the U.S. does spend much more, if more unevenly, on education than we skin-flint Canadians do. It's also a cultural thing, a reflection of certain social attitudes, a side effect of our differing anti-intellectualisms. Canadian anti-intellectualism is not quite as vocal as the U.S. version, and there is a little more respect for education in the Great White North. Part of this is a result of something old: Canada's Europeanism, much of which is a reaction against the mega-culture next door. Part of it is a result of something new: immigrants, who tend to push their kids to excel in school.

Canadians are generally more deferential than Americans, and therefore have more respect for those who succeed in the confines of established institutions. People are still mildly in favour of professors and science nerds, provided that they engage in wry self-deprecation. An intellectual cannot put on airs or come off like a swell. This is fatal in a land that loves to hack its tall poppies. So long as Canadian smarties act like secular monks, devoted to the greater good of research or their students, they're fine. Not as good as hockey players, not as loathsome as politicians, Canuck brains are largely out of sight and out of mind until they magic up a Canadarm or some medical doohickey and win a Nobel Prize and five approving minutes on the CBC. There is one exception to this rule. Illustrious foreigners, especially Brits and Americans, who choose to live in Canada have much more leeway to pontificate and greater licence to make pompous pronouncements. They're kind enough to grace this global backwater with their presence, so they can puff and brag a bit.

Americans are more inclined to emphasize the goods an education can get you, treating school as a means to an end rather than an end in itself. Consequently, the people who stay in school because they love the things they are studying have failed to reach the end, and are merely delaying the inevitable real world. American admiration of the self-made man or the rugged individualist means that scholastic success will always be a consolation prize at best, less worthy than starting your own company or inventing something. You can achieve the latter goals on your own, and the market determines whether or not they are successful, not some hoity-toity coterie of experts. It's hardly surprising that a culture that routinely derides academic prowess – as opposed to fiscal and physical expertise, the objects of collective worship – produces middling, bored students.

I'm not quite cynical enough to conclude that standardized testing is a deliberate dumbing down, a way to snuff brains out before they become perilously critical. I don't think that the people who come up with these accountability schemes are trying to make that Kurt Vonnegut story come true, consciously creating Harrison Bergeron–esque Community Handicappers. It's just another instance of the more-money-than-brains mindset at work, of our fondness for technical reason and rejection of other ways of thinking. Business lobby groups like Chambers of Commerce remain staunch supporters of accountability measures such as standardized tests. The exclusive focus on basic English and math suggests that the ultimate goal of school is training people to work, not teaching them to read and write and think and argue. All we really need to do is learn 'em so they don't frig up the cash register or offend the customers.

The other shitty thing about accountability schemes is that they drive a lot of teachers out of the profession. The Web teems with complaints from former instructors who tired of teaching to the test. This only exacerbates one of the real problems affecting public schools on both sides of the border: it's very difficult to recruit, train, and retain good teachers. Teaching has one of the highest attrition rates of any profession, with many leaving within five years. Some bitch about the mediocre pay, others complain about discipline problems in the classroom, but the most commonly cited reason for leaving the profession is intransigent and ineffectual administrators who undermine or overrule the teachers they are supposed to support.

Again, part of the problem is attitudinal. Teaching is treated, at best, as a default career, something middle class-ish but not as good as real moneymaking professions such as doctoring or lawyering. Teaching still suffers from being a feminized profession, a girl job, part of the pink-collar ghetto.

This is a hangover from the days when teaching was one of the few professions open to women. But a lot of those old lady teachers were tough birds and battle-axes, strict disciplinarians with high standards. Christ, my own grandmother once sent me to detention for accidentally calling her Nanny in class. She ruled the third grade with an iron fist.

Such discipline is no longer permitted by many school boards. Teachers now have much less autonomy than my Nanny did. The idea that teachers are simply glorified baby-sitters – and the old saw "Those who can't do, teach" – says a lot about the way we really value the profession that is the gateway to all the professions. This lack of status means that the best and the brightest, the really hardcore nerds, often avoid teaching careers.

Guess which college majors get some of the lowest scores on American college exit tests such as the GRE, GMAT, and LSAT? That would be the education majors. Even the hung-over popped-collar biz bros have better scores than America's future educators.[21] Which students get the highest scores on these exit tests? Everyone's favourite joke majors: philosophy, English lit, and humanities, along with respectable pursuits such as physics and math.

If the ed majors I've encountered are any indication, teaching does indeed draw too many not-so-scholarly young women who just looove kids but are not so crazy about learning. Kids don't need teachers to teach them how to be kids or to coo over how cute and special they are. These women should certainly open awesome daycares or have their own lucky broods. They're perfectly fine for the first couple of alphabet and number years, when kids should be having fun while they learn, but there is no way they should be responsible for grade 5, 8, or 12 English or science or history.

Caring about your subject matter is much more important than caring about the children. We need teachers who looove English or science or history, which is not always the case with ed majors. This is another real problem, one that starts with the way we educate our educators. Many choose to teach and then pick teachable subjects, which seems totally bass-ackwards to me. To be fair, universities often err in the opposite direction, hiring prolific researchers who have gone so far into Etruscan pottery or quantum physics that they can no longer remember how to explain it to someone meeting it for the first time. Those professors stink too, but they don't do as much damage as the teacher who is totally dependent on the answer key and discourages any deviation from it.

Standardized testing regimes, perversely, reward these uninspired, ill-informed "just following orders" teachers. This is pretty funny when you think of every beloved movie teacher ever. Hottie or zany charismatic or inner-city hardass, beloved superstar teachers succeed by making their own rules, by caring more about poems or the kids than The System, man. The public eats up this heroic teacher myth with a ladle. Then they vote for pols who push standardized schemes that ensure their fantasies will remain exactly that.

This isn't just movie myth, either. If you ask most people about their favourite teachers, they will usually describe a devoted weirdo or a classic disciplinarian, someone whose enthusiasm for the subject was infectious or whose willingness to impose stringent standards made it clear that learning matters. When people complain about the teachers they hated, you often hear about the boneheads who just repeated the textbook chapter and verse, who were unable to cope with any questions the book did not answer, who squelched the curiosity that drives genuine learning.

A bad teacher, or a system that encourages bad teaching, does serious damage to scores of kids. Happily, the reverse is true too; a couple of good teachers can help make up for a multitude of childhood challenges and set someone off in the general direction of a better life. I was lucky enough to have several really great teachers, arch-conservatives and radicals, old-school hardasses and eccentrics, who convinced me that teaching was the most awesome job in the world. I still feel that way. And I know a critical mass of other profs and teachers who feel the same way, and suspect that you might know or remember some too.

That is why, even though I am concerned about the deleterious effects of passive, overly testy education, I am suspicious of "school sucks" stories. They obscure real problems in the school system that could be ameliorated with political will and some cash. I don't want to make this sound easy-peasy; it's difficult to agree on educational standards, and even harder to implement and assess them. It demands a lot from parents, students, teachers, and administrators. But most of the people who cry public-school crisis have little interest in doing this kind of hard work. Instead they cry crisis to advance a political agenda that is usually anti-public and anti-school, anti-intellectual and anti-union.

Lest we forget, St. Reagan, when he was campaigning in 1980, swore he would destroy the Department of Education, a child of the Carter administration. That and the reinstatement of school prayer were the only education "issues" Reagan gave a toss about. A Democratic majority made his plan impossible, and then, in 1983, the report *A Nation at Risk* came out. Full of dire stats about poor performance in math, reading, and science, the report is heavy on Cold War gloom and doom: "If an unfriendly foreign power had attempted to impose on America the mediocre educational performance that exists today, we might well have viewed it as an act of war. As it stands, we have allowed this to happen to ourselves."[22] This is reminiscent of the previous education panic, the 1960s freak-out about Sputnik, the fear that the Russians would out-science and out-smart the West. Only this time, it wasn't just the commies. The Japanese, with their superior cars and students, were also gaining on America.

Every president since Reagan has made political hay of the school-crisis-speak we see in *A Nation at Risk*. Critics of the report allege that it was an unduly dire reading of indicators like SAT scores. But it is also very important to note that this report made little mention of standardized tests as a solution for problems in the schools. It had nothing to say about voucher systems or tax breaks or school choice, much to Reagan's chagrin. Rather, it recommended more demanding curricula, longer school days, and higher standards.

Education expert Diane Ravitch, who served in Bush I's and Clinton's education departments, says that *A Nation at Risk* is "the most important education reform document of the 20th century"[23] and argues that schemes like NCLB have totally betrayed its spirit and goals. Ravitch makes two arguments about school reform that I am very partial to. First, she points out that the focus on testing eclipses another, more widespread problem: the sheer shoddiness of many school textbooks.

State standards and publishing-house concerns about complaints mean that texts range from pap to just plain wrong. This is another one of those issues, like charter schools, where the antipodes of right and left meet. Ravitch contends that righties police offensive issues (evolution, sex) while lefties sanitize language (racism, sexism, Eurocentrism). Combine cruddy texts with teachers who are strongly encouraged to stick to them – or are too dependent on them – and you get kids who learn to hate reading and learning.[24]

Moreover, even though individual states defend the autonomy of their school systems, textbook content is often influenced by the states that place the biggest orders for books. The second-biggest textbook market in America is Texas, which is currently run by so-con right-wingers who have made approving noises about science texts with creationist material. They support striking Cesar Chavez and Thurgood Marshall from the history books and replacing them with the likes of Newt Gingrich, Phyllis Schlafly, Rush Limbaugh, Focus on the Family, and the NRA.[25]

The textbook publishing industry is making a mockery of the notion that each state has complete control over its curriculum. That brings us to the other part of Ravitch's analysis that I like. She supports a national core curriculum, and she has argued in favour of one for a long time. She would like to see a school system where "every student would have the opportunity to study history, geography, the sciences, the arts, literature, mathematics, and civics in every grade, with adequate time for physical education."[26]

When Ravitch was working for Clinton, she tried to institute national curriculum standards, but they died a messy legislative death. Many cited some of the same complaints that came up when Dubya passed NCLB, objecting to federal meddling in local matters. But so long as students eventually leave their Podunk towns, surf a World Wide Web, and are subject to the vicissitudes of a global economy, education is *not* a local issue. Education is an everybody issue, and it should be a national priority. Federal governments in the U.S. and Canada should be more actively involved in ameliorating two gaps: the funding gaps between affluent school districts and impoverished ones, and the curricular gaps between challenging schools and challenged ones.

Obama's secretary of education, Arne Duncan, has been speaking in favour of national standards, arguing that NCLB was too dumbed down and scattershot to work. Forty-six states have agreed to participate in the development of national standards, while the states that hate The State – Texas, Alaska, South Carolina, and Missouri – object to the proposal. But the dialogue about national standards is still being phrased in terms of accountability, school choice, and standardized tests. The conversation continues to be about narrow quanta, tougher tests, and more accurate measures of accountability.

Both the U.S. and Canada are made up of many different local cultures. But that is precisely why there should be national core curricula, so that inhabitants of diverse regions have some culture and facts in common. Ravitch asks, is math or Greek tragedy or the periodic table really that different in Louisiana and California, Alberta and Nova Scotia? No. Or at least, they shouldn't be.

The thing I like about Ravitch's approach is that she focuses on texts, not tests. Texts, not tests is a good place to start rethinking our approach to education policy, since it shifts the discussion from the usual narrow number-crunching to questions of quality. Which texts are must-reads for any educated American or Canadian? What scientific ideas and mathematical concepts, which historical events and artworks should we have in common? These are questions we could have some lively, long-overdue debates about, if only anyone had the political will to suggest that civilization matters, to insist that education is not merely a local and economic issue, but a national, ethical, and social one. But that would mean saying that people who read fare better than people who don't, and that some books are better than others. You can't say that on television or the campaign trail.

Rigorous national curriculum guidelines would help ameliorate the ignorance and anti-intellectualism wrought by patchwork standards, standardized testing regimes, and sappy self-esteem-inflating psychobabble. I am a firm believer in educational standards, but then, who isn't? The problem is that the standards that currently prevail aren't nearly educational or standard enough. If educrats and politicos, parents and voters were actually committed to education in any meaningful way, they would invest in better assessments of it than the ones a Scantron machine and a roomful of psychometric wonks can provide.

The Scantron is the robot brain that does much of North America's academic shitwork, grading student work automatically by skimming over their pencilled-in bubbles and spitting out a score. It judges student work without wasting any time reading or responding to it. Anyone who has taught knows that grading is the gruelling part of the gig, that it can take hours to correct a stack of papers if you do it right and show the students everything they are doing wrong.

I like evaluation systems that educrats would doubtless consider hopelessly antiquated and prohibitively labour-intensive. Bubble tests are a perfectly fine way to assess factual knowledge, but students should also be tested on their ability to make arguments, to write a piece of persuasive prose or explain a concept. There should be more essay-based exams, and oral exams too, but those require warm bodies, which require paycheques. The SAT recently added an essay component, but it does not deduct marks for grammatical errors or bad content, and the graders seem to award points on the basis of quantity, not quality. That's hardly an auspicious start, but essay-based tests are a step in the right direction.

Or we could always look to the East and the future. In 2009, Japanese researchers unveiled Saya, a robot teacher, and let her conduct classes at a Tokyo school. Saya can call the roll and mimic teacherly feelings such as sadness, anger, and disgust. It is highly unlikely that she will ever express any interest in organizing her fellow droids or criticizing whatever curriculum her programmers make her run. If we're going to let robots like the almighty Scantron do the grading, we might as well let them teach. We've already started driving the humanities out of the schools. Why not go all the way, and get rid of the pesky humans too?

Chapter Four

SCREW U OR HATE MY PROFESSORS

Colleges and universities are major economic engines,
while also serving as civic and cultural centers.

— *A TEST OF LEADERSHIP: CHARTING THE FUTURE OF U.S. HIGHER*
EDUCATION (A.K.A THE SPELLINGS COMMISSION REPORT)

When I was an irritating idealistic undergraduate, I thought everyone should go to university. My friends and I enthused about those super-civilized, culture-mad countries in Europe that charged no tuition, the ones where they would *pay* people to go to school – like learning was *important,* or something. Why, those lucky bastards probably got free wine and cheese too. Not like in dumbass, get-a-job North America, where college was simply a means to an end, a private benefit to be shilled vigorously like any other high-end product. Not like in dumbass, get-a-job North America, where any major that does not directly correspond to a professional title inspires choruses of derisive howls: "What are you going to dooo with that?"

I still retain a teensy shred of idealism. Anyone who is genuinely interested in learning should be able go to university. But a decade of teaching has beaten the shining egalitarian dream of universal access out of me. There are a lot of people in university who have no business being there. Classrooms are peopled with the doomed and the dragooned, with heel-dragging heaps of burning money and wasted time. Many students are unready, unwilling, or unable to do university-level work. I know it borders on blasphemy to say such a thing in a culture that works overtime to find new "intelligences" so everyone's kid can be special. But I've tried to teach plenty of students who had very little interest in learning, and much less in learning English. Why should larval nurses or engineers waste their time learning to read, write, speak, and think? Like, duh, they already know, like, English, y'know?

There are more university students than ever before. But as drink-soaked curmudgeon Kingsley Amis warned when the U.K. liberalized its universities, "more will mean worse." Concerned professional nerds wonder if popular success has come at the cost of standards and rigour, if the university has sold its soul to fill its seats and coffers. Rising enrolments have led to increased anxiety about the state and fate of the institution, if the shelves upon shelves of eulogies for higher ed and calls to restore it are any indication.

Despairing tomes about the ebbing vitality and integrity of universities in the U.S. and Canada abound, with titles such as *Declining by Degrees, The University in Ruins, Education's End, Ivory Tower Blues, No Place to Learn,* and the granddaddy of this genre, Allan Bloom's 1987 surprise hit, *The Closing of the American Mind*. I read my own weight in the damn things and then, to quote Dorothy Parker, I shot myself.

Leftish university-decline books generally place the blame on customer-service rhetoric and corporatization, and rightish ones bemoan lefty classroom indoctrination and the dissolution of standards and canons. Lefties also tend to argue in favour of universal access and increased government funding. Right-wingers contend that there are too many losers doing useless artsy-fartsy degrees already, and pitch market solutions. Both miss the mark.

The university sells students – and their parents – careers in its shiny brochures, on its ever-expanding websites. This is also the standard party line for guidance counsellors and high-school teachers. Go to college, get a marketable degree, and spend the rest of your life being cosseted by dropouts and arts majors. But this kind of credentialism changes the relationship between professors and students. If students are paying for the degree rather than the classes, buying a chit instead of a challenge, then I am not an instructor. I am a potential impediment, someone who might stand in the way of the future the university promised them. If I "take points off" – their words, not mine – for crappy work, then I may well inconvenience them. After all, the university promised them a product: jobs.

Credentialism, in concert with the customer-centric language universities now use to address their students, has effectively demoted professors to the nerdiest wing of the service industry. I am the students' employee – a grammar janitor, a language waitress. Good service means A's. Bad grades are bad service, a finger in your chili or a mouse in your beer, evidence that the help has fucked up again. Good service means classes that are entertaining. Bad service means classes that are boring or hard.

Credentialism has made some students quite cynical about the value of education, which helps explain rampant plagiarism, the flourishing online paper mills and the development of services such as Turnitin.com to surveil the problem. Students buy or steal work because they can, thanks to the Internet's new and improved cheat-friendly technologies. However, plagiarism also shows us that college is a system to be gamed, that the piece of paper matters more than the learning that piece of paper is supposed to represent.

Want to know how to get into college? It's pretty easy – write a cheque. Oh sure, you still have to work hard to get into a top-notch school, but the fair-to-middling majority welcome your patronage, regardless of your skill or dedication. Simply give them thousands and thousands of dollars and as far as Any University is concerned, you are fit for the rigours of higher education. If it is a "student-centred" university you'll likely squeak by, as your instructors will have been instructed not to fail too many of the customers. Don't want to prick their precious self-esteem! If it is not "student-centred," your school can let you flail around and flunk, which means it can make you take those classes again, and charge you again – *cha-ching!* In extremis, it may turf you for poor performance or plagiarism. But you can probably get back in on academic probation if you (natch) write another cheque.

Post-secondary education is a booming business indeed. Over the past couple of decades, what with nearly constant talk about the knowledge economy and the information careers of the future, post-secondary education has done boffo box office, which is especially impressive given that the institution is in crisis. According to the National Center for Education Statistics, U.S. college and university enrolment grew 14 per cent between 1987 and 1997. Between 1997 and 2007, it grew by 26 per cent. In 2007 approximately 29.5 million students were registered at colleges and universities.[1] And the experts say this number will just keep on climbing, if for grim reasons, as recessions often send people back to school to upgrade in search of better work. In Canada, 2007 figures also show that post-secondary enrolment has been growing, increasing 31 per cent between 2000 and 2006.[2] In 2007–08, according to the latest data from StatsCan, over a million students were enrolled in post-secondary education, a record high.

North American colleges and universities are putting more bums in the seats, and they are also charging a lot more for the privilege of snoring your way through Psych 101. Tuition increases have steadily outpaced inflation. In fact, financial aid counsellors say that tuition increases are usually double the rate of inflation. According to a 2007 study by the College Board, tuition costs in the United States jumped 35 per cent between 2000 and 2005. The average tuition at a public four-year college has continued to rise; in 2008–09 it was $6,585, while the average cost of tuition at a private four-year college was $25,143.[3] In Canada the average undergrad tuition was $4,724 in 2008–09.[4] Of course, none of these figures include the numerous student fees, the outrageous markups on textbooks, and the costs of niceties such as food and shelter, which contribute to big fat student debt loads.

Administrators and educrats say that the droves who continue to enrol are evidence that tuition increases are not a significant barrier to access. But what this actually shows us is that a college education has become mandatory if one aspires to the middle class or better. Kids of all ages are taking out mortgages on their brains because they have been told a million times that university is the only route to a decent job.

But post-secondary graduates are not impressing employers much. One report, conducted by the Association of American Colleges and Universities, found that 63 per cent of employers think college graduates "lack the skills to succeed in our global economy."[5] A study by business think tank the Conference Board called *Are They Really Ready to Work?* answers with a resounding no. Its authors write: "Only about one-quarter of four-year college graduates are perceived to be excellent in many of the most important skills, and more than one-quarter of four-year college graduates are perceived to be deficiently prepared in Written Communications."[6]

The employers surveyed by the Conference Board listed the most important skills that college graduates require to be work-ready. The top ten are

- oral communications
- teamwork/collaboration

- professionalism/work ethic
- written communications
- critical thinking/problem solving
- writing in English
- English language
- reading comprehension
- ethics/social responsibility
- leadership[7]

And then, at the very bottom of the list – in twentieth place – is poor ol' humanities/arts, which a piffling 13 per cent of employers rank as valuable. This in spite of the fact that at least seven of the skills they specifically request – things like reading, writing, critical thinking, and ethics – get more of a workout in the humanities and liberal arts than in any other program.

The employer types surveyed by the Conference Board have a reflexive disdain for the seeming uselessness of the humanities. Then they bitch and moan because college grads can't read, write, think, or speak very well. It doesn't take a lot of critical thinking or problem-solving skills to see the obvious contradiction here. No wonder colleges are failing, even by these bullshit boss-friendly, job-o-centric standards.

And here's a fun fact about the Conference Board: in May 2009 its branch in Canada had to apologize for three of its reports because they were plagiarized, hastily cobbled-together cut-and-paste jobs like so many fraudulent under-grad papers. The punchline? The offending reports dealt with intellectual property and copyright issues.

For employers, the ultimate elusive performance indicator of the success or failure of academia is how much they can save on training by sloughing off the costs onto colleges, students, and taxpayers. Reading, writing, and thinking matter because CEOs are peeved that their pedigreed underlings cannot bang out an email or a report. Ignorance is to be deplored, not for its deleterious effects on the body politic, public discourse, or our personal lives, but because it might inconvenience or embarrass management or adversely affect the bottom line.

But this assumption – that education is good because it equals mo' money – is precisely why many students cannot be bothered to learn how to read or write or think. They can't see how ethics or historical knowledge or linguistic skills might be of any use to them in their future careers. They grow impatient, annoyed by persistent pedagogical deviations from the end goal: getting paid.

The idea that universities should be career training academies, posher, better-appointed versions of DeVry, is one that goes all the way to the top in North America. After the economy started tanking in Canada in 2009, Prime Minister Harper floated a plan to divert funding from the Social Sciences and Humanities Research Council (SSHRC) to graduate students doing business degrees. This was exactly wrong. It wasn't the philosophers, historians, and sociologists that SSHRC supports who led us into fiscal peril. No, it was people with business degrees. Making it a political priority to fund more of them is like clinging to a chunk of the *Titanic* crying, "We shoulda built a bigger boat."

Obama has said that he wants to see every American complete some post-secondary education, but the first post-secondary stimulus funds went to community colleges and job training. The Bush administration also believed that university + college = job training, as we see in the Spellings Commission report quoted at the beginning of this chapter. The line describing universities as economic engines that are incidentally civic and cultural is a pithy summary of the report's ethos, its unwavering commitment to money over brains.

The Spellings Commission was Bush's attempt to initiate some NCLB-style "measuring is the gateway" accountability measures at the post-secondary level. The only disciplines that the Spellings report refers to are the STEMS: science, technology, engineering, and math. Save for a glancing reference to foreign languages, which are important because America needs to sell things to people who talk funny, the report makes no reference whatsoever to the humanities or liberal arts. Those terms don't appear once in seventy-six pages of buzzwords. Instead, we see thirty-six references to accountability, nineteen to consumers, sixteen to efficiency, and fourteen to employers.[8]

The conversion of universities into job-training centres, and the increase in college enrolment for that same reason, is seriously exacerbating our ignorance and anti-intellectualism. It should be the other way around. Higher levels of post-secondary education ought to lead to more lively intellectual debates, a greater respect for civilization and culture, and a more nerd-friendly public. The volume and vehemence of anti-nerd invective make it clear that this is not the case. It's a paradox worthy of Yogi Berra, like the club nobody goes to anymore because it is too popular. Put a B.A. on every wall and they become wallpaper. University has become a rite of passage rather than a right or responsibility.

The university has grown increasingly anti-intellectual, adopting the pragmatisms and populisms of the culture at large and increasing its roster of explicitly careerist programs. This only brings in more knuckleheads who should not be in university. This only creates more bullies who hate university and bash nerds.

Plenty of people enrol in college and end up failing to complete their degree or taking much longer than advertised to finish it. In fact, 42.5 per cent of American students who sign up for a basic four-year degree do not manage to complete it within five years.[9] There's an achievement gap here too, with a greater percentage of low-income and minority students taking longer to finish, or never finishing at all. (Again, as with K–12, Canadian students do a bit better, with only 15 per cent failing to complete.)[10]

Many students quit because they can't hack the cost, can't afford to pay tuition and lose income. Others cannot hack the classes and course work. Presumably these ex-students, who have little to show for their efforts but a heap of debt, bafflement, and resentment, dislike whatever reminds them of the tedious, useless life of the mind. The same is likely true of the students who managed to slide through on the least possible effort and see their E-Z degrees as proof that college is just a costly joke.

The university is one of the places where we see the love-hate relationship with knowledge very clearly. Whenever a post-secondary education story gets posted on the *Globe and Mail* or *New York Times* website, for example, trolls swarm the board, fulminating about cutting off their public funding. They rejoice at the thought of murdering every seemingly impractical discipline, hanging the last art history prof with the guts of the last philosopher, the better to serve science, engineering, and business, the only fields of inquiry that justify their existence with tangible benefits.

Or cranks get in a huff because fags, feminists, and radical minorities have seized control of the ivory tower. The other really loud complaint about universities is a political one. They, like the bathroom in that kitschy anti-commie poster, are breeding Bolsheviks, as the majority of professors in the humanities and sciences skew liberal-to-lefty.

Conservative columnist Barbara Kay, writing for Canada's *National Post,* went so far as to suggest that left-wing bias at universities was the most serious problem affecting the nation. Here's a smidge of her screed, which is typical of the genre: "From their ivory towers our leftist ecclesiastics rigorously monitor the four credos from which no dissent is permitted: relativism (each to his own 'truth' except the truth of relativism, which is absolute), feminism, postcolonialism and multiculturalism (cultures trump civilization)."[11]

You can find far less grammatical variations on these themes all over the Web. This is another of those get-you-coming-and-going-arguments, like the anti-nerd allegations listed in the first chapter. Do we believe in no truth, or are we radical activists for the other isms that we propagate as truths? Are we po-mo nihilists or politically correct true believers? Anti-Christs or new priests? And isn't civilization made up of, um, cultures?

To be fair, there are some leftist dogmatics in academe, surely as there are Tories on Bay Street or Republican millionaires in Texas. But if you think that this hardcore minority of tenured radicals are turnin' anyone not already that way inclined, you are paranoid. Boring doctrinaire leftists are lunch for Kay and her ilk. They goad a very special minority to become hot-headed doctrinaire rightists. And those students keep doughty right-wing columnists permanently supplied with column fodder, with tattletales and fresh outrages: *My prof said Stephen Harper was awfully chubby for a robot. Can we fire/sue/stone him?*

I may have lefty sympathies, but the last thing I want to see in a student paper is what I think. I make that very clear in every class I teach. I'm there to provide information and assistance, and it's their job to think, to come up with their own ideas and back them up with evidence or research. I don't grade them on what they think but how well they think and express it. And that's how most of my colleagues roll too.

It is awfully disingenuous for righty dogmatists to claim they are flying the flags for truth, objectivity, and science when they are incensed about other values such as God, family, patriotism, and capitalism. The constant righty slurs against relativism are lazy and sloppy, displaying an ignorance of the very tradition they pretend to defend. Relativism is not some sulphurous vapour from the seditious 1960s; it's been there all

along. Classical thought is not some marble temple of abso-
lutes. It includes sophists and the original cynics and skeptics.
Michel de Montaigne, the Renaissance thinker whom many
nerds call the inventor of the personal essay, was hardly
some po-mo nihilist. His essay "On the Cannibals" is a classic
example of a relativist argument: the people of the New
World may have some barbaric habits, but they have the
decency to eat dead men instead of torturing living ones in
the name of decency and religion like hypocritical Europeans.
Conservatives' kvetching about relativism is another expression of their desire for authority, their nostalgic longing for
the absolute wisdom of Big Dad.

I'm sympathetic to pleas to keep the university open and
genuinely liberal in the old John Stuart Mill sense. I just don't
think that's what most of these prof-bashing types are asking
for. Rather, they want some kind of conservative staffing
parity, one that would make the university subject to the
same shift – down and to the right – that we've seen in public
discourse and political life. Such complaints ignore the fact
that faculties such as business and economics swing the other
way politically. Then there are all those fundie schools, like
Liberty University and Bob Jones, where you can skip all the
secular hedonism and stick to the English that was good
enough for Jesus.

The right presumes that scores of conservative nerds
are getting blacklisted from academia by the commissars of
correctness. But analysts have argued that the liberal majority in the arts and sciences is the result of a self-selecting
process driven by the personal values that influence

political ideologies. A paper by the husband-and-wife – and Republican-and-Democratic – team Matthew Woessner and April Kelly-Woessner looked at the different factors that influence students in favour of grad school and academia, including liberal bias. They argue that self-identified conservatives are more interested in having families and making money, whereas self-identified liberals and lefties value creativity, flexibility, and doing meaningful work more than money or babies.[12]

Consequently, conservative students tend to cluster in the professional faculties, which are more likely to result in money and babies sooner rather than later. Lefty libs do enjoy a slight edge in the professorial schmoozing sweepstakes, but the differences between lefties and cons are statistically insignificant when it comes to grades and professorial support. Furthermore, both ideological camps clean the clocks of self-described moderates, who do worst of all. This research was presented at the very conservative American Enterprise Institute, in conjunction with a conference called "Reforming the Politically Correct University." The Drs. Woessner do argue that keeping the classroom apolitical, or balanced, might help incubate more conservative grad students, but they also advocate liberal policy initiatives to close the con gap: better pay and more family-friendly workloads.

The most high-profile figure in the anti-lefty-prof campaign is David Horowitz, who has cranked out countless op eds and a couple of books about the scourge, inventorying the U.S.'s most scurrilous socialists and tenured radicals. *The Professors: The 101 Most Dangerous Academics in America* is precisely that, a shit list of the leftiest lefties in all of academe, an omnium-gatherum of the most egregiously anti-American honky-haters, Palestinian-huggers, eco-feminists, and unabashed Marxists.

A former lefty radical himself, Horowitz is very adept at using progressive language to serve his retrograde cause, couching his campaign in terms of intellectual diversity and plurality. This means that he and his fellow-travellers in the right-wing media and think tanks, the very people who bitched longest and loudest about quotas and affirmative action, are now demanding quotas for conservatives. The people who shat a brick about campus language codes and anti-discrimination policies are now trying to craft them. It's a political twist analogous to the Creation Museum's use of Enlightenment trappings to advance anti-Enlightenment beliefs.

What is the logical extension of calls for political parity on all academic issues? Business profs forced to assign socialist critiques of the system as a counterpoint to their steady diet of "yay for capital"? Medicine profs giving equal time to crystal healing and homeopathy? And why stop there with the sensitivity to delicate student sensibilities? Should my English syllabus ditch the divine Emily Dickinson and replace her with the latest chick lit out of respect for the differently literate or the poetically challenged?

Of course not. This isn't about learned judgments but ideological ones. Some groups have even gone so far as to declare that they will be monitoring and recording professors, searching for more scary, traitorous quotes. In 2008 the conservatives at the National Association of Scholars announced they were starting something called the Argus Project. Just like that

Greek mythology guy all covered in jeepers peepers, so too shall conservative scholars have eyes on campus as volunteers scrutinize the nation's colleges to see if anyone conducts "politicized teaching, requires ideological adherence, or sustains slights to conservative students."[13]

Any reasonable person will recoil at the sight of phrases such as "requires ideological adherence," and no responsible prof, regardless of his or her ideological stripe, would request such a thing. Required *factual* adherence is quite another matter, though, and that's where this issue gets quite swampy, when groups such as creationists also cry academic freedom in defence of their nonsense.

The word that really slays me, though, is *slights*. It's pretty paternalistic and patronizing to assume that a thinking adult, or at least somebody who has expressed an interest in becoming one by signing up for higher ed, cannot hear opposing or critical views without getting the vapours or feeling brainwashed. This charge also assumes that students are too dumb to recognize ideological bias, even though they fairly marinate in it while watching TV or surfing the Web.

Once we get the professors on a short leash, do we monitor student-on-student slights too, like when Chomsky Junior gets into a nasty dust-up with Mr. College Conservative in their political philosophy seminar? You can't have the totally neutral or balanced college that right-wing rhetoric romanticizes unless the students come to college ideologically pristine, untouched by their parents' steady diet of Fox News or BBC World, or their peers' interest in kicking Iraqi ass or saving Darfur.

I've spent time on both sides of the campus divide that professional alarmists like Horowitz keep conjuring, which is why I find so many of the right wing's claims wildly exaggerated and pointlessly polarizing, statements that exist for the express purpose of enriching the speaker by inflaming everyone else. I have walked among the bow-tied and the Birkenstocked, the monarchists and the Marxists. I've studied and taught the Great Dead White Men they recommend and the po-mo studies they revile as sophistry in the service of sedition and sodomy. Not once did anyone shave my head and shame me like a Vichy traitor for serving both sides of the culture wars.

There aren't many Horowitzian anti-extremist extremists. Much of this "grassroots movement" for students' rights is Astroturf, artificially kept alive on Fox News and talk radio, louder than it is large. These groups' websites hardly teem with popular outrage. No Indoctrination.org has collected a measly 178 complaints in the past seven years. Students for Academic Freedom, Horowitz's super-fun student fan club, no longer has a forum to report ideological abuses. Last time I saw it, there were around four hundred complaints, some of which were obvious goofs, such as people saying that their economics prof was indoctrinating them with capitalism. Then there were some malcontent loons claiming, "they woodnt let's me into aPHD," whose issues are more personal than political.

Students love bitching about their profs on the Web. Rate My Professors has amassed millions of gripes from the disgruntled students of many lands. In the summer of 2009, the site celebrated cracking the ten-million-reviews mark. Many universities and student unions have launched their own professor-review websites and guides. There we see students complaining about things that bother them more than any sort of perceived bias or attempted brainwashing. They savage hard markers, heavy foreign accents, favouritism, and bad dressers, dissing the grouchy and the incoherent and the dull and the unfair and the not hot.

Arguing that ideological bias is the most serious problem afflicting our universities perpetuates two ideas that hurt our capacity to consider ideas: namely, that every truth depends on your political persuasion and that there are only two sides to every argument. The fancy technical term for this is bi-univocal, and the best example of it is the news. Show the protestors and the anti-protestors, a head that says yea and another that says nay. Teach evolution *and* creationism! Equal time for all, regardless of evidence, relevance, or import – which are antiquated and elitist notions, or crafty cover for activist agendas.

Horowitz buries the lead and misses a real problem in his rush to assemble his festive bonfire of straw men. In a foot-note in *The Professors,* he talks about how he never heard this kind of political indoctrination when he was a student at Columbia College in the 1950s. He writes, "There was a reluc-tance to look at events more recent than twenty-five years in the past because of the dangers of 'present-mindedness' and the fear that events so fresh could not be examined with 'scholarly disinterest.' "[14]

Times have changed. We prefer fresh ideas and new break-throughs. Twenty-five-year-old ideas happened before many of our students were born. They will probably be uninterested, not disinterested in the scholarly way that Horowitz intends. The university's current "student-centredness" combined with inadequate student preparation in the K–12 system has condemned us to the present, so we are often stuck in a cul-de-sac of current events. This means a lot of talk about pop culture and contemporary issues, even when a prof is trying to teach an old text. And it isn't just the kids who are stuck in their own cultural moment. The disciplines are suffering from the same presentism too. In a 2008 editorial called "Gone and Being Forgotten," UCLA professor Russell Jacoby wonders where all the old thinkers have gone. People aren't reading Hegel in poli-sci or Freud in psych; instead, they're reading the latest theories and research.[15] These fields are behaving as though they've been promoted to the hard sciences – yet another sign of our tendency to treat technical reason as the only worthwhile form of thought.

Here's a gem from the Spellings Report that exhibits the same relentless presentism: "We recommend that America's colleges and universities embrace a culture of continuous innovation and quality improvement."[16] This is the misshapen issue of Stalinist crop projections mating with management-speak. Are philosophy, history, and literature fields in which one witnesses "continuous innovation and quality improvement"? Not really. Scientistic – not scientific – notions of constant improvement and innovation are utterly at odds with any thoughtful study of our past. Given that the university is one of a handful of institutions that maintains a connection to the past, it is all the more distressing to see this presentism and scientism at work in academia.

The liberal arts are not just old; they are also accused of being weird, and deliberately so. Humanities professors are routinely derided as professional obscurantists and obfuscators, traffickers in snooty jargon. To cite just one example, when revered French thinker Jacques Derrida died in 2004, the supposedly liberal and brainy *New York Times* ran a dismissive obituary of the "abstruse" thinker that incited the ire of professional nerds all over the world. Derrida's obituary was merely the latest in a long line of anti-theory screeds. In short, the message is "This shit is hard on purpose and it makes no sense!" Deconstruct the Western tradition and the Gray Lady spits on your grave. Deconstruct the global economy and she reports your latest multi-million-dollar bonus.

I concede that there exists some dreadful, deliberately prolix academic writing. That's inevitable under publish-or-perish rules in a weak job market. But the subtext here is blatantly anti-intellectual. It says that philosophy and literature profs are only faking it, putting on airs, when they produce work that is difficult or complex. Literary and philosophical thinking dare not outpace common sense or popular taste.

Conversely, the sciences, because they are a form of technical reason, have the right to be as complicated as they wanna be. Nobody ever blusters about the physics department, castigating the way their needlessly elaborate equations spurn the understanding of the common man. Nobody demands transparency from the chemistry department because their complex formulas might grow up to be pills or pantyhose or explosives, y'know, like, things people can use. When it comes to, like, words, and the, like, meaning of stuff, everybody's got a write 2 they're opinion and no body's better then any buddy. Who teh heLL R u 2 tEll me what 2 reed or how 2 spel?

The activities at the very heart of the university – reading and writing – get demoted to gen ed requirements or electives that round out "real" subjects like business and hotel management. Students approach them with all the vim and vigour that the descriptors *general* and *mandatory* usually elicit. That single required English course or philosophy elective that Useful Studies majors are frogmarched through then gives them the right to dismiss such disciplines as fluff, to wave away thousands of years of human endeavour as nothing other than preparation for a career in front of a deep-fat fryer, har-dee-har-har.

We treat university education as another consumer good, a product, not a process. University rankings such as the ones generated by *U.S. News and World Report,* or the Canadian version in *Maclean's* magazine, always sell really well. People love a list. But the rankings also show us the conflicting missions of the university. They imply that a college education, like any other consumer good, is easy to review and rank. But when universities question them for this very reason, academia gets thwacked with the public-service, taxpayer-accountability stick. Post-secondary education is stranded in a weird limbo somewhere between being a public service and a big-ticket purchase.

Some liberal arts colleges, such as St. John's and Reed, have long refused to participate in the *U.S. News and World Report* rankings, arguing that they encourage educational homogeneity, stat gaming, and status seeking. In 2006, eleven Canadian university presidents announced that their institutions would not participate in the *Maclean's* survey, citing concerns about the way the magazine weighted and packaged the data they submitted. Lest you surmise that this was merely sour grapes from the losers, the letter's signatories included top-ranking schools such as the University of Toronto. Their actions emboldened another fifteen schools to drop out.

Undaunted, *Maclean's* has continued to put together its guide using publicly available data. Its editorial about the boycott began, "Nobody likes being graded, particularly those used to giving tests, not sitting them,"[17] spinning the universities' arguments against their methods as a refusal to submit to scrutiny. It sounds good, but the people used to giving tests and grades had to take a shitload of tests and get a gazillion grades themselves before they got to grade or test anyone else. Most of us remember how it feels. (Some of us even *like* it. Sick, I know.)

The grading certainly does not stop when profs start grading others. There are peer reviews that will determine whether they publish or perish, endless grant applications, and piles of files for tenure and promotion reviews. At the end of almost every course in North America, the students get to grade their instructors too, filling out little Wendy's comment cards rating their professorial expertise, helpfulness, and so forth on a scale of one to five.

Nerds are hardly strangers to scrutiny. Universities love to crank out performance indicators and metrics and studies about themselves. They form associations to create new surveys and studies. They regularly poll the kids and the profs and the alums. Many of the universities on both sides of the border that dropped out of the college rankings have made piles of stats available on their websites. The problem is making this tide of info legible for non-experts such as high-school students, workers who want to take some classes, or parents, to present this information in a way that strikes a balance between specialist wonkery and marketing puffery.

I'm not saying the university is above or beyond scrutiny. It may be my favourite place, but several criticisms of the university are totally legit. Let's start at the beginning. Many first-year classes are cash cows that treat students worse than cattle; at least future burgers get free drugs. If you're sitting in a theatre with several hundred other people looking at PowerPoint slides straight out of some overpriced Psych 101 textbook, then you are being ripped off. And at the worst possible time too.

Given the gap that looms between high school and college-level work, it's absolutely unconscionable and counter-productive for universities to leave students stranded during their frosh year. But that's when the kids take the really huge prerequisite lectures they need to qualify for something that's more like teaching and less like a cheesy motivational speech.

We could fix this with rigorous – and affordable – transition-year programs, sort of like Quebec's CEGEPs. Give every student a basic grounding in reading, writing, humanities, and sciences. Throw in some practical things like fiscal awareness to keep the real-worlders happy. Get the gen ed in at the beginning rather than in piecemeal electives that are too little, too late. This would provide a more structured and supportive introduction to the university or, for that matter, community college.

A transition year could serve as a bridge, allowing wafflers to sort themselves into college and community college slots. Departments of both institutions would ideally have a chance to tell students what they're all about before they enrol there, only to drop out. And we could certainly run evening and weekend versions of such programs too, in order to accommodate the growing numbers of working adult students. We could even give them some sort of credential at the end, something to take up that awkward space between high school and a B.A., between under- and overqualified for crappy-to-middling work. At least students would have something to show for their efforts other than successful completion of a pile of multiple-choice tests or becoming part of the universities' annual mass cull.

The most popular college major in America, according to the nice people at the *Princeton Review,* is business, a practical, get-a-job program that does not belong in the university at all. Business programs are relative Johnny-come-latelies; the first one, the Wharton School at the University of Pennsylvania, started in 1881. The collegiate business school did not really catch on in Canada or Europe until the middle of the twentieth century. It is now a popular major in Canada as well, ranking just behind social sciences and law, which tie for first place on the list of most popular majors, and just ahead of health and education, the third-place winners.

If I were Queen of the Colleges for a day, the first thing I would do is burn down all the business schools and salt the ashes so no more M.B.A.-lings could spring up from the ruins. Then I'd torch public relations, leisure studies, hotel management, and every other career-training program, until all that remained at the university were the truly academic disciplines, namely the hard sciences, the social sciences – yes, that includes economics – and the liberal arts. These fields of study all offer something other than practical applications and ways to make a buck. If the university wants to survive as an intellectual institution, it must slash and burn the professional suburbs to save the theoretical town.

In all seriousness, we should transfer the primarily practical, get-a-job programs, such as business schools and faculties of public relations, to the community college system. This would also have the salutary effect of removing the outdated blue-collar stigma from community colleges. A muchness of ink has been spilled about the acute shortage of skilled tradespeople in Canada and the U.S. The idea that white-collar jobs are the only good jobs, and that university is the only way to get them, is part of the reason why we have too many bad students and not enough good plumbers.

The kind of person who goes to school because he wants to make a lot of money in managing or marketing has much more in common with people who go to school because they want to make a lot of money being electricians. They are at school for the same reason: to get a credential and the technical skills that qualify them for a career. The nerds, conversely, are there out of love for a specific discipline, a love that seems silly and self-indulgent to stolid money-minded types.

Of course we still need to train businesspeople and hotel managers. And I'm not saying their work isn't complicated too. But the key word in that sentence is *train,* and training is not the same as teaching. Training means instructing students to do something specific, like marketing or accounting or welding. Teaching is all about developing broader skills, such as argumentation or experimentation, by looking at specificities that may well seem useless, like the literature that ate my youth or the protein my biochemist pal pursued for years. Those subjects might have some useful applications eventually – teaching, medical research – but that is not why we squandered our twenties in libraries and labs.

It is unlikely that its administrators will raze the toniest suburbs of the bloated, sprawling metropolis that is the contemporary university. I have no doubt that they will do the exact opposite and continue to generate more anti-academic, anti-intellectual job-training departments. We might as well just hang up big signs that say "Boss Studies" or "I Love Kids" or "E-Z Computer Jobs Here" and make things totally student-centred. Moneyed entities will continue to endow chairs in however they made their fortunes so that franchising and hawking take their places of honour beside the shrivelled husks of philosophy and history.

Administrators aren't going to turn down donations or fees to preserve the tiny, quaint town squares that spawned the university, the places that look backwards and hold on to the old. No dean or recruiter will ever encourage students who signed up for job training and got English lit and Rocks for Jocks to go elsewhere, to where their aspirations and talents might be better served.

Students are also subject to another pernicious bait-and-switch. The university sells teachers, but it hires researchers and then pushes them to produce, which means they spend less time teaching. Enter the grad students, part-timers, and assorted adjuncts who do most of the teaching, particularly in those first few sink-or-swim years of study. In the U.S., for example,

> Three decades ago, adjuncts – both part-timers and full-timers not on a tenure track – represented only 43 percent of professors, according to the professors association, which has studied data reported to the federal Education Department. Currently, the association says, they account for nearly 70 percent of professors at colleges and universities, both public and private.[18]

There aren't any comparable recent Canadian numbers. The last time StatsCan counted, back in 1998, there were 28,000 part-time profs and 34,000 with tenure. But Canadian universities have since persuaded the federal bean-counters that it's too dang hard to keep track of the adjuncts who come and go.

Does any school really want to 'fess up and let parents and students know how many of their costly classes will be conducted by greenhorn grad students and "roads scholars" or "freeway flyers," who teach a bunch of different courses on different campuses to cobble together a meagre living? Teaching matters sooo much to deans and admincritters that they are willing to pay someone approximately one tuition fee – if they are lucky – per class per term. Some U.S. schools pay as little as $1,000 per class per term. If there are thirty students in that class, they should receive approximately $33.33 worth of expert attention apiece. Surely the business types would approve of such an efficient apportionment of teacher attention. But do you think Any University U.S.A. will include that figure in their promotional brochures and web pages?

It's easy to see the values of the contemporary university. Just take a stroll through your friendly local campus and look at the buildings. There's always cash for a new dorm or a new stadium, since benefactors like to slap their names on those. Mall-ish food courts are common. I've never set foot in a business building that wasn't state of the art, from the floors to the chairs to the classroom tech. Conversely, I have taken and taught liberal arts classes in mouldy rooms strewn with trash in the wings of the university that nobody bothers to maintain, since nobody wants to donate a Bigwig Memorial Mop-and-Paint Job.

All the angry talk about elite institutions existing at a luxurious remove from the "real world" is risible. Does a tenured prof at Yale or U of T have a sweet ride? Sure. But they are at the tippy-tippy top of their fields, and investment bankers of like rank would laugh at the paltry sums nerds consider good money. Moreover, the really high salaries at universities go to non-academic types such as management and athletic coaches.

Most college and university instructors in North America are harried, underpaid contract or part-time workers, just like many of their students. Both groups are short on money and time, busting their humps in pursuit of a promotion that may never arrive. Ivory tower, my arse! This sounds exactly like the mercenary shit-show that the commonsensical call the "real world."

Universities hire more contingent workers because they're cheaper and because they can, as there are more Ph.D.'s and M.A.'s than there are real jobs, particularly in the humanities. Some boomers are finally aging out of the profession, as promised throughout the 1990s, but they aren't going to retire as quickly as people think. Just look at the way they've prolonged Rolling Stones tours and their erections beyond all seemliness. Even when they do retire or die on the job, their exodus is often seen as a great opportunity to convert costly tenured positions into cheap part-time work and to recruit the starriest research stars to fill the few spots that remain.

The starrier the stars, the less likely students are to see them, as they must maintain their school's place in the firmament. These stars may well be great teachers too, but they will likely spend more of their time on the road or in the lab than with students. Research hauls in money – private and public – and prestige. There is not much room on the tenure track for people who prefer teaching and would rather spend their time working with students than proving themselves to their peers. Hiring committees do consider teaching philosophies and student evaluations, but there is always the suspicion that someone might garner high ratings from the students for the wrong reasons, like being a snappy dresser or an easy grader.

The number of books and papers published and grants successfully snared are more reliable, objective indicators. "Publish or perish" is evidence of the quantitative mania at work in the humanities. Hiring committees hardly have time to read all those articles candidates list in their cvs. They are doing more administrative work, thanks to the university's increased dependence on part-timers, and they have to write their own articles and books for people to not read so they too can level up.

The teaching that most prospective students and parents think they are paying for just doesn't pay. Part-timers who focus on teaching do so at their own peril. And the perverse economy of the university too often rewards profs who think they are too good to teach, who would rather impress their guild than help their students.

I'm not impugning academic research *tout court*, but the fact that it is a must – the only road out of adjunct serfdom – means there are a whack of forced and futile verbiage and stacks of stupid studies out there. And those heaps of rarely read journals and books only confirm the use-minded's dismissive preconceptions about the liberal arts even as they strain to conform to their quantitative standards.

Universities are cutting their library book budgets in favour of more tech, which means fewer guaranteed university press sales and more people trying to cram their tricked-out dissertations through an increasingly narrow bottleneck.

Lindsay Waters, the former humanities editor of Harvard University Press, argues that the publish-or-perish model is bad for books and the humanities. He writes, "there is a causal connection between the corporatist demand for increased productivity and the draining from all publications of any significance other than as a number. The humanities are in a crisis now because many of the presuppositions about what counts are absolutely inimical to the humanities."[19] The useless studies have a hard time measuring up to the standards of the useful studies because they have different ends and advantages, ones the use-minded dismiss as imaginary or irrelevant.

Training is wrecking teaching. Budding nerds have been overrun by people who are in college so they can be somewhere else. We've poured a bucket of water into a bowl of soup, so neither constituency gets the nourishment it needs. Or, to put this in more dramatic terms, the humanities are occupied territory, ruled by hostile foreign powers that have run them off their own native turf. If we can't measure "humanity" in the same way that standardized tests assess intellect or M.B.A.-lings measure profits, then it is a meaningless category, one unworthy of sustained inquiry. People should sort out what being humane means on their own time and their own dime.

I could monetize this argument and point to the scores of liberal arts graduates who eventually do well, or contend that culture is a powerful economic engine. But I don't want to make this case on Gradgrindist grounds, to twist things around and insist that useless school can turn out to be really useful after all. That is true, but it is not my point.

The useful studies – because they are nothing more than useful – are pale shadows of their elderly relatives in the useless studies. The useful studies are puffed-up training programs, job descriptions masquerading as academic disciplines. The more the merely useful encroaches on the university, the harder it gets for the seemingly useless to survive there. And where else is all that useless beauty supposed to live? I suspect the answer to this question, for many cost-cutters and real-worlders, is another question: *who cares?* If there is no more market for ancient Greek, there should be no more ancient Greek. If there are no jobs for historians, there should be no history. If there is no money in brains, there should be no brains – except for the brains that make money.

Chapter Five

BULLY VS. NERD

On the Persistence of Freedumb in Political Life

⁓

BALLOT BOX: The altar of democracy. The cult served
upon it is the worship of jackals by jackasses.

— H.L. MENCKEN[1]

A snoozer conference: Last night's primetime news conference,
President Obama's fourth since taking office, was as much a
dry health-care symposium as it was a give-and-take with
reporters. Honest question: Is there a point when the
president knows too much about an issue?

— CHUCK TODD, NBC'S LEAD POLITICAL CORRESPONDENT[2]

When Barack Obama won the 2008 U.S. election, many pundits argued that his victory was a repudiation of the incompetence and anti-intellectualism of the Bush years, a sign that the public longed for smart leadership. "Brains are back!" declared Michael Hirsh, *Newsweek's* Washington correspondent. Obama's victory marked a return to rationality and pragmatism. Hirsh reported: "Sun Belt politics represented by George W. Bush – the politics of ideological rigidity, religious zealotry and anti-intellectualism – 'has for the moment played itself out,' says presidential historian Robert Dallek."[3]

Hirsh's column ran in November, right after the election, when the world entire was abubble with hope. In the intervening months, we have all learned just how stubborn the politics of rigidity, zealotry, and anti-intellectualism really are. Republicans may be in the political minority, but rump status has only made the right's remnants louder and crazier, more strident and emotive.

Throughout 2009, Fox News bloviators, gaggles of disgruntled crackers, and a handful of Republican politicos gathered for "teabagging" parties where they protested the taxation and tyranny of the new administration. Some even went so far as to don Glenn Beckian Founding Fathers drag, while others mailed teabags to their representatives or dumped tea in local bodies of water, a gesture that shows their lack of respect for all things public, including historical accuracy.

Throughout the summer of 2009, when members of Congress and senators held town hall meetings to discuss the administration's proposed health-care reform plans, the question-and-answer sessions degenerated into hooting and hollering, boos and bellowing. Prune-faced honkies and fresh-faced LaRouchies eschewed questions in favour of conspiratorial nonsense and paranoid fear-mongering, baying that health care was un-American, likening the President to a Nazi, a commie, and a fascist.

In his August 2009 town hall, John McCain was asked the following by a member of Arizona's considerable old-bag constituency: "I would like to know how the President's getting by ... with all this money ... it's against the Constitution. Doesn't he know it's against the Constitution?" This indignant mess was greeted with many cheers. When McCain replied, "I'm sure that he does ... I'm serious. I'm sure that he respects the Constitution of the United States," he was rewarded with yowls and jeers.[4]

As many of you are doubtless already aware, before he started his career in politics, Barack Obama taught constitutional law at the University of Chicago for more than a decade. Dude has forgotten more about the Constitution than these anti-government grumpuses will ever know. I'm no constitutional scholar, but I do know that the preamble says the government has a duty to "promote the general Welfare." The very first power of Congress is to collect taxes to ensure a common defence and, again, the "general Welfare." Moreover, wing-nut favourites like the army and the navy appear near the bottom of Congress's list of powers, below nerdy priorities such as promoting the "progress of Science and useful Arts" through copyright law.

Here's another significant passage of the Constitution, one that the right has flouted shamelessly for as long as I can remember: "No religious Test shall ever be required as a Qualification to any Office or public Trust under the United States." Of course, given that these chuckleheads can't tell the difference between Nazism, communism, and liberal democracy, things that the Constitution actually says are beside the point. None of the protestors, to my knowledge, ever specified which parts of the Constitution Obama was traducing. The rhetoric of the right-wing protests bore little resemblance to the legal, procedural language of the Constitution, sounding a lot more like the fiery fuck-the-King polemics of the Declaration of Independence. The pseudo-populist right are sore losers and drama queens who think the other side's winning a majority and trying to fulfil a central campaign promise is exactly like the "long train of abuses and usurpations" meted out by a distant foreign tyrant.

The right-wingers who once equated anti-Bush sentiment with treason did a *volte-face* on respecting the office of the POTUS once that smart black guy took office. When Obama addressed America's schoolchildren in September 2009, angry parents cried indoctrination and some school boards refused to air the speech. Florida GOP chairman Jim Greer declared, "As the father of four children, I am absolutely appalled that taxpayer dollars are being used to spread President Obama's socialist ideology."[5]

Obama's speech was more little red schoolhouse than little red book, an endorsement of conservative values such as hard work, personal responsibility, and trying your best. Laura Bush supported him, and even Greer conceded that the speech was not as Trotskyist as he had feared. Of course, some right-wing pundits spun this as a victory for their side. If they hadn't intervened and pitched a hissy, they said, the socialist prez woulda been quoting Castro. Never mind that Obama has given many a work-hard-and-stay-in-school speech, voicing values that are much more conservative than the reactionary vitriol and apocalyptic doomsaying of his opponents.

The right tried to spin the school speech as an unprecedented exercise of executive power, but the first Bush and Reagan did the exact same thing. When Reagan delivered his address to students in 1988, it was unabashedly partisan, enthusing about the joys of tax cuts and less government, arguing that the Republican way was the American way, which was swiftly becoming the way of the world.

Many of his tropes – his fulsome praise of free enterprise and the Founding Fathers, for example – still inform right-wing rhetoric. The anti-government mantras of the tea-party and town hall types are stale, dumbed-down Reaganspeak, right down to the red scares that played so well at the ass end of the Cold War. And those red scares were repeats anyway, cover versions of McCarthyism. These folks have not changed their minds in more than twenty years, but their ideas have changed America, for the worse, causing many of the problems they now complain about.

Dubya's experiments with untrammelled Reaganomics were an abject failure. His administration racked up the debt and trashed the economy. Some conservatives, to be fair, have distanced themselves from the former regime for that reason. But the hard right, the reactionary lumpenyanks, continue to worship the holy trinity of tax cuts, defence spending, and deregulation, in spite of all the wreckage they have wrought. Dubya's disasters were insufficient to disprove their beliefs. They blame not the ideas but the man, claiming that Bush wasn't really a true believer. Once he got to Washington, he sold out, succumbing to the siren song of big government. It wasn't that Bush was too Reagany. He was not Reagany enough. There can be no such thing as too Reagany for the reactionary lumpenyanks who "want *their* country back." If they could vote for his mouldering corpse, they would.

Obama is not their president. And though there were plenty of vile racist signs at tea-party rallies, I do not think that race is the only thing that makes him appear foreign and threatening to the teabaggers and town hallers. They believe Obama is illegitimate because he represents the unreal America – brainy America – and there hasn't really been a leader from around them parts since JFK. Obama can burnish his Midwestern niceness all he likes, but his suspiciously mellifluous speech and cerebral demeanour make him a usurper. He is a Manchurian candidate from the fifth column of educated city folk who gleefully grind virtuous small-towners under the heels of their modish, overpriced jackboots.

The anti-tyrant yawping was proudly and vociferously anti-intellectual. Obama, the nerd-in-chief, and learned health-care wonks such as Harvard's Dr. Ezekiel Emmanuel were cast as sinister experts who want to control everything, heartless technocrats who long to dispatch Grandma to a death panel. Reason once again appeared as cold calculation rather than ethical deliberation, as a purely technical antagonist to basic human decency, which dwells in the heart, not the head.

Pundits and PR hucksters used hot-button phrases such as "government takeover of health care" to exploit elitophobia, anti-intellectualism, and the anti-government streak that has always been part of American politics. Anti-health-care types also invoked other anti-nerd myths, alleging that any public health-care plan was sky pie, wildly unrealistic, and way too expensive, something that might work in Europe, but never in the real world. At the same time, the payload of stats and research from every other industrialized country, which shows that their public health-care systems are more efficient and effective than America's private system, was dismissed as socialist propaganda, more phony liberal expertise. It is ideologically impossible for certain Americans to admit that any government can do anything right, a belief that inspires unintentionally hilarious outbursts such as "I've been on food stamps and welfare – any one help me out? No!"[6] and "Keep your government hands off my Medicare!"[7]

The fact that the President had to stoop to conquer the persistent rumour that the gub'mint was going to kill Grandma is a testament to two things. First, there really is no bar and no bottom to political discourse. Powerful lobbies and private interests have the wherewithal and the willingness to muddy the waters. They distribute whatever low-down, illogical, and just plain unhelpful slogans and distortions their buzzword technicians recommend to maintain their profit margins. Second, there are many less fortunate foot soldiers, grunts who are happy to repeat these free-market mantras to sow panic about shadowy gub'mint bureaucrats and their nefarious schemes, for pleasure and for profit. Sure, some of the town hall protestors and teabaggers were just independent dittoheads and freelance racists, but others were Astroturf organized by corporate-whore lobby groups such as FreedomWorks, former Republican Congressman Dick Armey's dick army.

The panic over public health care is funny and sad, since America has had death panels and sinister bureaucrats for years. They're called Aetna, Humana, and WellPoint, and they make a killing, figuratively and literally. Protesting on their behalf is like making a charitable donation to Wal-Mart or sending a fruit basket to the CEO of the bureaucracy that fired you or foreclosed on your house. Nevertheless, "severely normal" Americans turned out to defend the status quo, to uphold the constitutional right to gouge sick people, ration care, and generate massive profits. If Aetna is no longer free to make a pile of dough denying Grandma's suffering, then no American is truly free, and the Marxist Nazi Muslims win.

I can understand why Republican pols repeat this codswallop. They do it for the same reason high-class escorts praise aging executive schlongs – that's what the people renting them have paid for. The same is true of the Blue Dog Democrats. What is more disheartening is that the Democrats who do support a health-care plan are also constrained by the power of big donors and by public hysteria about big gub'mint.

Even Obama had to use the free-marketeering lingua franca of competition and choice to pitch his plans, which shows us that Americans still trust the market and money more than they trust the government or brains. The health-care "debate" is yet another example of the economic elite using the intellectual elite as a distraction, a cartoon villain, to conceal their own perfidy and retain their power. Universal health care would be a victory for brains, so the money-minded are duty bound to defeat it by any means necessary.

The health-care debate is just one example of broader trends in North American politics. You have to love the entertainment value, if not the probity or efficacy, of a political system that requires its candidates to sell out to moneyed interests *and* invest the proceeds in waterfront property on the moral high ground. This is not a contradiction so much as it is a commitment to two different kinds of private value, one moral and one fiscal. North American politics has become resolutely anti-public, driven as it is by two private engines: personal values and private wealth.

This has rendered North American political life idiotic, in a very old and specific sense. For the ancient Greeks, the idiot was the totally private person, the person who did not participate in the public life of the polis. The term wasn't necessarily derogatory; *idiot* meant something more like "common man" or "worker," and was closer to *particular* than *selfish,* as we see in other *idio-* words like *idiosyncratic* and *idiomatic.* It picks up pejorative heft throughout the history of the West, as when Marx praises the unprecedented productivity of the bourgeoisie for rescuing so many people from "the idiocy of rural life."[8] The word was enlisted by the medical profession in the eighteenth and nineteenth centuries as a descriptor for retardation, lingering in *idiot-savant,* a term that has lately been decommissioned and replaced by *autistic savant.*

In the twentieth century, *idiot* stumbled out of the clinic and into its current gig as an all-purpose smear, one that gets a lot more work than *cretin* or *mongoloid* but is less offensive than *retard*. Right-wingers are fond of employing "useful idiot" – their phrase for communist Russia's Western appeasers and apologists – to suggest that anyone liberal or lefty is an ally of totalitarian forces. Lefties tend to use it in the more generic, whatta-maroon sense while mocking chicken hawks who can't find the places they wanna bomb on a map.

It doesn't matter what your party affiliation is. We all live under idiocracy, insofar as we have become a people with little sense of the public good, people whose politics are largely devoted to personal or private issues. A candidate's faith or fidelity to his family or ability to seem like an all right dude is a crucial qualification for office. And once the winner takes office, his highest task will be a largely private one as well: responsible stewardship of the economy and the prompt return of tax dollars to their rightful owners.

Tax cuts are a good example of a very popular policy that is idiotic in the sense that I intend. Despite all the tea-party tantrums, Obama has actually cut taxes, like many other leaders who are trying to stimulate the moribund economy. And tax cuts were equally popular when we were in merry mid-bubble. Bush and Cheney bet that people like tax cuts better than balanced budgets, and they won a second term. Tax cuts are now a permanent plank in every party platform, in good times and bad.

Tax cuts are also declarations that the public sector has failed and owes the people a partial refund for services poorly rendered. It's like a restaurant comping you a free dessert to make up for an overdone entree. Here, citizens, take this coupla hundred bucks back; you know far better than we do how best to spend your cash. We fucked up and we give up. Most tax cuts are just shrugs, politicians abdicating their civic responsibility as leaders and then wrapping their laziness in flattery and bribery.

Alleging that someone is a "tax-and-spend liberal" sounds absurd to me, like saying that someone is a "teach-and-grade professor" or a "tackle-and-catch-the-ball football player." Deciding who and what to tax and what programs to invest in represents a goodly chunk of the work of governance. Instead of making long-term investments in public infrastructure such as roads, schools, and hospitals – the kind of resources that allow all of us to exercise our freedom – tax-cutting governments give voters chump change and try to purchase our loyalty with relatively minor private perks, with idiocratic short-term rewards. Everyone can count the cash and enjoy it immediately; you can't say the same for the kind of long-term benefits bestowed by good schools, bridges, or novels.

Tax cuts have become a campaign staple, a constant promise, whether or not those cuts conflict with other assurances about balanced budgets or spending. It is impossible for politicians to promise anything but fiscal conservatism, and equally impossible for them to deliver anything that vaguely resembles it. And if we can't make government work at this bean-counting level, the one our leaders keep emphasizing, it is hardly surprising that people can be quite cynical about the prospect of the government's enacting measures that go beyond balancing the books and paying voters off with dribs and drabs of their own money.

Canadians are slightly less anti-tax than their southern

neighbours, largely because of health care. However lousy the current incarnation of the government may be, we can still go to the hospital for free, so we've got that going for us, which is nice. But anti-tax sentiment in Canada has grown more and more vocal as we have lurched to the right too.

From 1998 to 2002, Prime Minister Harper was president of the anti-tax National Citizens Coalition, which militates in favour of "more freedom through less government." The NCC, one of Canada's oldest right-wing groups, was founded in 1967 by an angry insurance executive opposed to Trudeaupian notions such as universal health care and a guaranteed annual income program. The NCC happily disseminates the pro-rich opinions of its wealthy members, assuring the public that they would be better off trusting plutocrats than politicos. It opposes all the usual public targets, such as the CBC, unions, and taxation in its many pernicious forms.

It's not as though Harper merely had a youthful dalliance with the radical free-market right. He went from being president of the anti-government NCC to leader of the opposition to prime minister in the time it takes to get a worthless B.A. Harper is but one of North America's cadre of idiocrats who preach anti-government governance until they form the government. They criticize executive power until they wield it, and they demand accountability and transparency until they are the ones who have to provide it. People who do not believe in public service, because they do not believe in the public sector, run for office in bad faith. *They're gonna take the system down from within, maaann.* But these pols are ultimately more interested in destruction or obstruction than genuine reform. Who tries to fix something they don't believe in? Can you imagine a computer company run by a guy who thinks we were better off with the abacus? A vegan steakhouse chef? Anti-government politicians are just as oxymoronic, and much more common, alas.

Heal thyself, idiocratic politicos. If the private sector is so fantastic, so much better at everything than the government, then *go join it.* Leave the work of governing to people who actually believe that governments can work. Quit besmirching your precious free-market principles, feeding your own photo-op families filthy federal funding. If the milk of the state be poison, detach thine own gums from the chapped taxpayer teat.

Nobody likes paying taxes. Nobody likes government waste. It's dead easy to campaign against those things, to promise that you will keep providing the services people like, plus wars, minus anyone having to pay for anything. Here's a telling moment from a 2008 campaign-trail stop in Aspen, Colorado: a *Washington Post* reporter noted that "McCain drew a smattering of laughter when he said 'I have to be against tax increases, as you know.'"[9] It was funny because it was true, one of those moments of McCain candour. No Republican or Conservative can propose tax increases of any sort, since that would contradict their fundamental message: that government itself is a waste.

If liberals float tax increases, they must couch them, as Obama and Bill Clinton did, as taxes on the very wealthiest, taxes that will not impose further burdens on the beleaguered middle class. But these promises are belied by the fact that

Democrats – and Liberals – also need to endear themselves to wealthy campaign contributors and lobbies. And no matter how modest the proposed tax increase, right-wingers accuse them of communism, any tax being a precipitous slippery slope to Soviet Russia, to punishing success. How dare the libs imperil North America's most precious national resources, our super-rich?

The relentless focus on the economy and tax cuts, seeing the government as a private wealth manager rather than the public infrastructure that ensures people are free to create wealth, is the most obviously idiocratic strain in political life. Radical idiocrats go even further, arguing that the government is nothing but a parasite battening on the free market's lifeblood. Such arguments ignore the contributions the public sector makes to private industry. I'm not even talking about the obvious corporate welfare or bailout packages. Good luck making or selling anything, or employing anyone, without roads and cops and a legal system, without the kind offices of schools and hospitals. There are more high-end spas and better snacks in socialist Sweden than in the libertarian paradise of Somalia.

Idiocracy is isolationist and interventionist. It demands that the government leave the people alone but it also asks it to punish the enemies who scare or offend them, such as Muslims, illegal immigrants, and gays. Idiocracy insists that economic choices should be private and individual. But it also allows private values, such as fundamentalist Christianity, to fill the space where a public ethic, a set of shared priorities, should be. It is idiocracy that ultimately binds the fiscally conservative and socially conservative wings of the right. Issues such as gay rights and abortion, the red meat of the so-con agenda, turn private, you-and-your-lover/doctor issues into public boondoggles. To put this another way, idiocratic politics demands that bureaucrats stay out of banks and boardrooms but invites them to crawl into our beds and classrooms.

Idiocracy is not confined to the right. The right hates the mainstream media and considers journalists another vile, verbose elite. But the mainstream media are also predominantly anti-public, more interested in pursuing private angles – what's in this for you? – or the personal lives of public figures. The coverage of political candidates as celebrities, the attention devoted to their families, hobbies, church attendance, tastes, and style, is not new but it has undoubtedly increased, and it is also idiocratic.

The anti-intellectual faction in politics has been emboldened by idiocracy. There is a lot of overlap between anti-government sentiment and anti-nerd invective. Anti-intellectualism has also become a more vocal and shameless part of political life thanks to technological advances and cultural shifts.

Television has played a part in this. While it does allow more people to see the candidates in action, it also shapes their campaigns, whittling them down to a series of skirmishes, scandals, ads, and sound bites. The Internet's effects are equally ambiguous – half awesome, half awful. The Web allows people access to an unprecedented amount of information about the candidates, but a lot of that info is bad. Gossip and fear-mongering circulate freely between the two screen worlds as the mainstream media investigate Internet controversies from heavy-on-the-caps chain emails, dignifying rumours that Obama is a "sekrit Muslin" or the Anti-Christ by trying to debunk them.

The Clinton camp, the McCain campaign, and anti-Obama reactionaries have all alleged that the media were in the tank for Obama from day one, that the press handed him his victory on a bed of valentines. And while I recall much gushing about Michelle's outfits, Obama's dandling skills, and various moving speeches, I also remember pundits repeatedly saying that he was just too stereotypically intellectual to win. Talking heads on both sides of the aisle made frequent use of the term *professorial*. It wasn't a compliment. For the Republicans, this term was a slur, a way of saying that Obama was condescending, dull, long-winded, and too busy thinking to act. For the Democrats, *professorial* was a constant concern, arousing fear that their candidate would seem too abstract and aloof and calmly and rationally explain himself right out of the race.

The American public has been flip-flopping about smart leaders for years. As Richard Hofstader argues in *Anti-intellectualism in American Life*, nerd-bashing fluctuates, comes and goes in cycles. Hofstader begins his analysis with the 1952 election, when Eisenhower trounced the "egghead" Adlai Stevenson. Hofstader quotes a speech Eisenhower delivered in 1954, in which he offered the following definition of an intellectual: "a man who takes more words than are necessary to tell more than he knows." This sounds a lot like a Reagan joke or the campaigns Hillary Clinton and McCain ran against Obama.

Hofstader's description of the caricature of the intellectual is also all too familiar. He writes:

> Intellectuals, it may be held, are pretentious, conceited, effeminate and snobbish; and very likely immoral, dangerous, and subversive. The plain sense of the common man, especially if tested by success in some demanding line of practical work, is an altogether adequate substitute for, if not actually much superior to, formal knowledge and expertise acquired in the schools.[10]

Recognize this pitch? It's the Reagan and Dubya sell, even though they were hardly rugged, self-made men. This was also the argument against candidates such as Gore, Kerry, and Obama. The right lambasted Gore for claiming that he "invented the Internet" and cast him as a green con man profiting from another elitist lie: global warming. The Swift Boaters torpedoed Kerry's service record and post-Vietnam protests, bending the facts to fit their wimpy weasel story about the Democratic candidate. The right made fun of "John François Kerry" for speaking French. They made fun of Obama for not serving in the military, and for speaking well.

Again, this is not new. Richard Nixon's anti-intellectualism was evident in his appeals to the Silent Majority and his fulminations against those no-goodnik college war protestors. Both are still favourite gambits of the Fox News/Reform Party faithful. Nixon's VP, Spiro Agnew, also did a brisk trade in anti-intellectual apothegms, like this doozy from a 1969 speech:

"A spirit of national masochism prevails, encouraged by an effete corps of impudent snobs who characterize themselves as intellectuals."[11] *Effete? Impudent?* Spiro's own vocabulatin' sounds pretty snobby compared to contemporary Republican discourse, just as Nixon's policies seem downright liberal compared to Reagan's or Dubya's.

The Nixon tapes are heavy on two antis that ride shotgun with anti-intellectualism – anti-Semitism and anti-gay invective. Kenneth J. Hughes, the tapes editor at the University of Virginia's Presidential Recordings Program, describes Nixon as a conspiracy theorist with three nemeses: "Jews, intellectuals, and Ivy Leaguers."[12] This paranoia and resentment, among other unsavoury qualities, drove Nixon to his downfall.

It also looked like shit on TV. This is one of the reasons why Reagan was such a vast improvement. He was able to reissue and repackage Nixonian anti-intellectualism with sunny smiles and catchy quips and optimistic bombast about America. Reagan, like Nixon, made his bones during the red scare. Also like Nixon, he made political hay out of college anti-war protests, inveighing against the decency and morality deficit in California's university system and the threat posed by "beatniks, radicals and filthy speech advocates." Reagan also said that universities should not be "subsidizing intellectual curiosity," which became policy when he became governor; he slashed the university system's budget and killed free tuition in California.[13]

Reagan's victory in 1980 marked the beginning of an ideological shift, a turning against government and nerds. He borrowed a lot from the anti-government themes that are

part of America's founding documents, but he also main-
streamed and normalized notions that loitered on the John
Bircher fringes of the right wing. William F. Buckley used to
say that it was important for the conservative movement to
police itself, to keep the kooks out in the interest of preserving
its political legitimacy. But Reagan was not so discerning, and
his successors proved even less picky.

Reagan helped the right position itself as the party of
ideas, outflanking the brains on their own turf. Speaking to
the Conservative Political Action Committee in 1985, he said:

> The truth is, conservative thought is no longer
> over here on the right; it's the mainstream now.
> . . . The other side is virtually bankrupt of ideas.
> It has nothing more to say, nothing to add to the
> debate. It has spent its intellectual capital, such as
> it was. . . . We in this room are not simply profit-
> ing from their bankruptcy; we are where we are
> because we're winning the contest of ideas. In fact,
> in the past decade, all of a sudden, quietly, mys-
> teriously, the Republican Party has become the
> party of ideas.[14]

Reagan was able to give greed some much-needed gravitas,
to compare the excesses of coked-out stockbrokers to the
freedoms extolled by the thinkers of the Enlightenment and
their Classical antecedents. The Reaganites presented their
America as not merely exceptional but downright world-
historical, Hegel directed by John Huston guided by Jesus,

starring a twinkly-eyed amalgam of John Wayne and Jimmy Stewart.

Approving wallets in the business community and their think tanks did indeed manage to yank the idea mantle away from nerds and heap fresh calumny on those in the learned professions. *Ha ha, we have the money and the brains! And what nerds know just isn't so.*

Republican Party ideas – strong defence, deregulation, tax cuts, trees causing pollution – were admittedly new after years of Democratic notions such as the New Deal and the Great Society. Now, nearly thirty years later, we can see the damage done by the ideas Reagan popularized with a grin: billions wasted on defence spending, soaring budget deficits, increased concentration of wealth, market instability, tattered public infrastructure, and brazen contempt for governance.

As his biographers have noted, Reagan developed most of his ideas before he came to power. This helped give him that air of glorious certitude that idiocrats mistake for moral conviction. That helped, but his ideas were also successful because they were so simple and there were so few of them. Conservative commentator and former Reagan speech-writer George F. Will explained: "The key is to understand the economy of leadership: you should have ideas, and they should be clear, but most of all they should be few – three at the most. Re-arm the country, cut the weight of government and win the cold war."[15]

The Reagan revolution, and Dubya's remake of it, did not curtail the bossy sweep of government or reduce spending. Quite the opposite. But Reagan's success certainly did shrink the language of leadership. It has ground down the sound bites, has truncated and circumscribed political discourse. Now it is very difficult to suggest complex solutions to complex problems without sandblasting policy proposals down to quippy inspirational Reaganisms.

The quote from Chuck Todd that opened this chapter suggests that even lead political correspondents from "liberal" media bastions such as NBC cannot bear too much information. A president who knows too much, who waxes wonky, risks putting his audience to sleep. American leaders, even the eloquent ones, must limit themselves to the kind of one-liners that look great superimposed upon a graphic of a flag and an eagle, just like the Great Communicator did.

The biggest cheers at the moribund 2008 Republican convention were for footage of the painted visage of Ronaldus Magnus that was spliced into nearly every video. Reagan presented himself as a crusader for truth, but he never met a fact he couldn't wave away with a myth or an anecdote or a misremembered scene from a movie. When someone called him on one of his many big baloneys – that the British hanged people for murder for simply owning guns – Reagan laughed it off and repeated it in a *New York Times* interview years later. As one of his aides said, "Well, it's a good story, though. It made the point, didn't it?"[16]

Reagan's successors have tried to replicate his pseudo-populism with varying results. George H. W. Bush didn't do a very good job of concealing his patrician preppiness or his long tenure in Washington, but he still impugned his rival Michael Dukakis for being too Harvard. He also warned that

Bill Clinton and his Oxford chums favoured "the false certitude of social engineering fashioned by a new economic elite of the so-called best and brightest. The best and the brightest are right out here in Middle America where you know what's going on."[17]

Clinton was able to get away with having a brain because his intellect was sheathed in reassuring Big Mac–munching bubbatude. He might have been a Rhodes Scholar, but he had a Reaganish ability to play himself in town halls and on MTV and talk shows. He was also the first president who seemed to be a product of the 1960s rather than the reactionary backlash against it. But the 1960s also had an anti-intellectual streak, which has lingered in the touchy-feeliness of the liberal boomers and Clinton's emoting on their behalf.

Boomers like Clinton talk a good game about social justice and congratulate themselves for changing the world in the magical 1960s. However, when they became the establishment, they did a swell job of serving and joining Team Money. Boomers had the good fortune to grow up during the greatest economic expansion in North American history, but they have ensured that generations X and Y will never, ever suffer the same corrupting affluence. Clinton managed to balance the budget, which is more than you can say for the economic wizards of the right, but he also left some ticking fiscal bombs behind. He passed disastrous fiscal deregulation such as the 1999 Gramm-Leach-Bliley act to placate the obstinate Newt Gingrichians in Congress. He let Greenspan run buck-wild. The problem with this kind of Third Way centrism, with saying shit like "the era of big government is over," is that it concedes the centre to the hard right and makes responsible governance look like some lefty fringe notion.

Boomer emoting such as Clinton's "I feel your pain" is anti-intellectual, just like Reagan's quips and Dubya's appeals to patriotism. Some boomers still cling to a hippyish Rousseau-for-Dummies belief in the natural goodness of people and the deleterious effects of the system. But they *are* the system, and have been for several decades. The notion that every child is special and that school systems should build every precious snowflake's self-esteem is a good example of squishy, sentimental liberal anti-intellectualism at work. And this feel-good rhetoric is consistently belied by self-centred boomer behaviour like voting for tax cuts that beggar the schools.

There are also some paranoiacs on the far left whose fantasies are just as baroque and implausible as the fascist takeover fables of the hard right. I'm thinking here of those who believe that 9/11 was an inside job, a conspiracy theory shared by some leftists and libertarians. But 9/11 truthers vastly overestimate the Bush administration's competence; they're simply pushing a lefty version of the nerds-control-everything myth.

No one party or creed has the monopoly on conspiracy theories or idiocratic ideas. But I don't want to be totally equivocal about this, either. False equivocation – the insistence that every issue has two equal and opposite sides – is what allows tea-party loons and town hall yellers to pass as one side of a health-care debate, a debate they are heckling and obstructing. The anti-intellectualism of the left is not as fervent, or as well-financed, as the anti-nerd invective of reactionaries out to slay liberal dragons like the New Deal and the Sixties.

Clinton's win just the beginning of a new battle. Private investment funded busy muckrakers who dug up his dirt and flung it all over the hill. The result? A ridiculous, costly desecration of the public sphere. A bunch of peckerwood prudes, most half as smart and some twice as slutty and sneaky, hoisted Clinton on his own petard: the hedonism that helped "humanize" his brains. Monicagate was an anti-governance triumph, private values walloping the holy heck out of public concerns, and a perfect example of idiocracy in action.

Dubya was a consummate idiocrat. His scorn for the scholarly is well-established, so I shall confine myself to just one example of it. He loved to talk about his gentleman's C's, particularly when he found himself in the company of nerds. As he famously said in his 2001 commencement address at Yale, "To those of you who received honours, awards, and distinctions, I say, well done. And to the C students I say, you, too, can be President of the United States."[18] He also used this joke to kid members of his own administration, which fairly bristled with doctorates. In 2007 he told reporters at a press conference, "I like to remind people that, like when I'm with Condi I say, she's the Ph.D. and I'm the C-student, and just look at who's the President and who's the advisor. (Laughter)"[19]

Some see this gag as folksy self-deprecation, but Bush is not mocking himself. He's making fun of nerds. This is not humility but bombast. Even though he was surrounded by a phalanx of Ph.D.'s such as Dr. Dick and Dr. Condi and Dr.

Wolfowitz, Bush aggrandized himself and his base by deni-
grating expertise in general. What this joke really says, to bum
a phrase from *The Simpsons*' Ralph Wiggum, is "I beat the
smart kids, I beat the smart kids."

The 2008 campaign was a veritable orgy of nerd-bashing.
Throughout the primaries Hillary Clinton tried desperately
to smear Obama with his smarts and use his eloquence as
evidence that he had nothing else to offer. What match are
pretty words for experience and deeds? Once the presidential
contest got underway, Republican and Democratic mouth-
pieces started lobbing E-bombs at each other. Who was the
real elitist? The rich guy or the smart guy? The guy with too
many fancy houses or the one with too much fancy talk?

The McCain campaign repeatedly maligned Obama for
latte-sipping snobbery, arugula-eating arrogance, and pusil-
lanimous Poindexterity. A Fox News correspondent sneered
at a photo of Obama riding his bike: "Where is he going . . . to
get a pocket protector for his nerd pencils. What *is* that?"[20]
The deficits Obama's critics listed were revealing. He had
never been the CEO of anything, nor had he toiled in some
branch of the military-industrial complex. One snide release
from the Mitt Romney camp said that he had never run so
much as a corner store.

For an opportunistic Reagan robot like Romney, making
piles of money is synonymous with leadership. Laying off
thousands of workers, as Romney did when he was with Bain
Capital, is real-world experience. Helping laid-off workers
retrain and find new jobs, as Obama did when he was a community organizer, is not.

Republicans spent their whole convention taking shots at Obama's work as a community organizer. This was code for "black radical who will redistribute your income to inner-city welfare queens." It was a strategic blunder; when you insult community organizers, they organize their communities. Tellingly, hardly any of the marquee speakers at the RNC bothered to mock Obama's academic career. Teaching constitutional law was beneath contempt, unworthy of a snarky snicker.

The McCain campaign team made their commitment to pseudo-populism very clear when they unveiled his running mate, Alaska governor Sarah Palin. Alaska has fewer citizens than many American cities and it is a negative-tax state, floating on a sea of oil revenues and federal funding. Like most red states and benighted backwater burgs, it continues to exist thanks to the taxpayer largesse of those shiftless blue states and cities full of snobs and sodomites. You'd never know that to hear Palin flap her glossy yap, though.

State-subsidized crackers love, love, love to lecture everyone else about self-reliance, small government, and being a decent, hardworking citizen. There's no snobbery like reverse snobbery. Palin's debut speech at the Republican National Convention was part sap, part vitriol, and all cornpone oversimplification and disdain for complexity. At her rallies, besotted hordes chanted "U! S! A!" as if she were wrestler Hacksaw Jim Duggan. The right-wing press anointed her the second coming of conservatism, the shapely love child of Reagan and Thatcher. Rush Limbaugh summed up Palin's appeal succinctly: "Babies, guns, and Jesus! Hot damn!"[21]

Moreover, as the right pointed out ever repeatingly, Palin, unlike Obama, had been the boss of something. Those somethings might have been a tiny town and a sparsely populated state, but she *ran* those suckers, goddammit. Being a boss – especially an autocratic, my-way-or-the-highway one – and leading a people are the same thing, or so says idiocratic politics.

Here's a blast from Palin's past, from an analysis of her mayoral term that appeared during her gubernatorial run:

> Palin has cited her mayoral work as a central part of her qualification to serve as governor. But at the beginning of her term, asked by the local newspaper how she would run the city without experienced department heads, she made the job sound like no big deal: "It's not rocket science. It's $6 million and 53 employees."[22]

As Porky Pig said, "Th-th-th-th-that's all, folks!" The government is a business, a budget, and some bossable staff, nothing more. Throw in McCain's talking points and you get the full picture. Government is a business and a war machine. (Hey, kids, guess which is which! Sorry, trick question.)

The Palin pick was a ploy that failed. She is not as popular as she was before she kept on talking. But the fact that a very ardent minority still believe she is their dream candidate demonstrates how persistent anti-intellectualism is. Palin is a perfect and pure idiocrat, opposed to any government she does not run, and her enduring popularity is an affirmation of idiocracy.

In an interview with the *Washington Post* in September 2008, McCain's campaign manager, Rick Davis, conceded that Palin was a deliberate curveball, a swerve away from the issues. "This election is not about issues," Davis said. "This election is about a composite view of what people take away from these candidates."[23] Palinmania was a way to circumvent any serious public debate about the economy or the war or the environment. The Republicans tried to turn an election that was already chockablock with private minutiae into a character campaign, a clash of personalities, a celebrity horse race between Palin and Obama: feisty MILF vs. uppity negro, bully vs. nerd.

Barack Obama may say encouraging things when he speaks of public trusts like health care and education, but he still had to promise middle-class tax cuts galore and play a cool dude on TV to win the election. Personal stories, the "narrative" pundits kept gabbing about, mattered more than policy positions. Here's an example of this kind of storytelling, an exemplary piece of anti-nerd invective.

In an August 2008 article in the righty publication the *American Spectator,* a commentator argued that the box-office success of *Batman: The Dark Knight* and Rush Limbaugh's new multi-million-dollar contract were indisputable proof that John McCain would win a landslide victory, for Batman, George Bush, Rush Limbaugh, and John McCain all play similar roles. They are heroic warriors on brave crusades who cannot be swayed by others' opinions. McCain, like Batman, is

> a rebel against the Establishment. He is unafraid to act. He is willing to take risks. He could not possibly care less about what "feels good" or whether anything he says or does "makes sense" to a single other person. He runs on instinct. He is here to do the right thing. Nothing more, nothing less.[24]

In the bizarro world of right-wing pseudo-populism, a millionaire superhero, a millionaire ex-prez, a millionaire professional gobshite, and a millionaire senator are not members of the Establishment. No, they are a ragtag band of righteous rebels sticking it to the Man.

Here we see once again that action and thought are mutually exclusive and thinking is for pussies. Unlike Obama with his foppish "sense-making," manly menfolk like Limbaugh and McCain "act on instinct." You know who else acts on instinct? My cats. And though I laugh whenever my feline cohabitants bash their heads against closed windows in pursuit of errant birds, I expect better from people – and much, much better from presidents and prime ministers.

The political promotion of thought and action as opposites, the valorization of guts and heart at the expense of the brain, has had dire consequences domestically and internationally, economically and politically. And it is not an exclusively American phenomenon either. The Great White North also suffers from idiocratic politicking.

The Harper Cons have repeatedly nerd-bashed Liberal leaders Stéphane Dion and his successor, Michael Ignatieff, mocking their academic bona fides as if Harper were some hewer of wood and drawer of water, a hardy pioneer portaging his way through the economics department of the University of Calgary. Harper's master's degree is not as perilously professorial as the Liberal leaders' Ph.D.'s, but it is wonkier than Bush's M.B.A. or the customary law degree.

Harper is a nerd who aspires to bullydom. He keeps his caucus on a short leash. He speaks to the public via ads. The press and the people – the ingrates! – cannot be trusted to stay on message. Like the American right, which Harper has long admired, he sees other parties as enemies. Such partisanship is unhelpful in a parliamentary system where the current Conservative minority government must negotiate and compromise with several parties to get anything done. Harper's preferred themes are tax cuts and law and order, and his public statements are rife with bullyspeak such as "strong," "tough," and "proud." Wrapping him in a fuzzy blue sweater vest and having him wax avuncular before a fireplace or tickle the ivories at the National Arts Centre only adds another layer of fake. He's a nerd wrapped in a bully trapped inside a sensitive Beatlemaniacal dweeb.

Harper, Dion, and Ignatieff are all too void of charisma, too visibly and audibly nerdy to run for American political office, let alone win party leadership. One might surmise that Canadians, like Europeans, are more tolerant of politicians with academic backgrounds than Americans are. But nearly all of our prime ministers have been lawyers, a category that encompasses both flamboyant, brainy sorts like Pierre Trudeau and money-minded corporate collaborators like Brian Mulroney.

Here is a fun fact: American politicians are actually better educated than their Canadian counterparts. Only 66 per cent of members of Parliament have an undergraduate degree, versus 93 per cent of the representatives in Congress.[25] The myths about socialist Soviet Canuckistan aren't accurate either, as the majority of Canadian MPs come from the private sector. Conversely, most U.S. representatives come from other state and local governments; they are part of a political class. U.S. politicos stay in public service far longer than their Canadian counterparts. Parliament has a much higher turnover rate than American political institutions do. This creates an amateurish, short-sighted political outlook, one that rarely sets its sights higher than the next election.

For all their differences, the U.S. and Canada share a democratic egalitarianism that is admirable in principle. Unfortunately, it blows in practice. We condone all kinds of inequities, economic and social, but enforce absolute equality when it comes to public displays of intelligence. No polity, or politician, has the latitude to be much smarter than the most ignorant citizens. The wording and inflections differ on the two sides of the border, but North Americans share similar idiocies and anti-intellectualisms, the same more-money-than-brains mindset.

The Canadian way of phrasing this attitude is "Who do you think you are?"(to borrow a title from the amazing Alice Munro). Canadians love to remind the presumptuous that they are no better than the rest of us. Robertson Davies used to tell a story about being at a party where someone announced that Prime Minister Lester B. Pearson had won the Nobel Peace Prize. An annoyed fellow reveller declared, "Who does he think he is?"[26] This most Canadian of questions is simultaneously reproachful and passive-aggressive, accusing its objects of thinking they are so frigging great.

The American version is more aggressive, defensive, and individualistic; it sounds like Travis Bickle's "Are you talking to *me?*" Where the Canadian version focuses on the offending snob and chides him for transgressing community standards such as mediocrity, the American one emphasizes the speaker's independence, his God-given right to his own opinion. *That snob has some nerve, thinking he is the boss of me!* The old "Don't tread on me" flag goes double for experts, and triple for government experts, who have no right to occupy your interior or exterior space or clutter it with their phony facts.

On both sides of the border, pseudo-populists convince the electorate that someone can be too smart for high office. In Canada, all one need do is invoke the spectre of Pierre Trudeau, the last unabashed intellectual to serve as prime minister. What did all his fancy book learnin' get us? Buncha debt and some stupid social programs! In the U.S., a panoply of lobbies, think tanks, and jesters like Limbaugh and Beck keep pouring the old anti-nerd wine into new bottles, getting their audiences ugly drunk on outrage, hopped up on their own anger and fear, thirsty for pitchfork vengeance and simple solutions.

The crazy thing about our idiocratic politics is how much expertise and intelligence go into keeping the bar low and the sound bites small. A staggering amount of research and polling, vast wonk machines of experts in sciences pseudo and actual, have devoted their copious smarts to the electioneering process, to crafting the perfect piece of terrifying bullshit sure to drive soccer moms in preferred zip codes to the polls to defend their darling sprogs.

All that expertise and intelligence is devoted to making politics more idiotic, more anti-intellectual. These experts assume that people cannot, will not understand the issues, so they must tell stories and stoke fears. Long-time political journalist Joe Klein writes:

> I am fed up with the insulting welter of sterilized speechifying, insipid photo ops, and idiotic advertising that passes for public discourse these days. I believe that American politics has become overly cautious, cynical, mechanistic, and bland; and I fear that the inanity and ugliness of post-modern public life has caused many Americans to lose the habits of citizenship.[27]

The scores of consultants who try to focus-group every candidate to maximal inoffensiveness – or strategic nastiness against the right wrong people – make the process less informative and more emotive. And the American campaigns that Klein covers are clown-car-packed carnivals compared to the stultifying small-mindedness, petty dramas, and hoary rhetoric of Canadian politics.

Knowing how to campaign, how to leverage the party platform as the national brand, matters a lot more than knowing how to govern. Canadians may think that our shorter, quieter elections are a sign that we are more sensible and marvel at the expensive spectacles down south, but most Canadian parties just keep on running for office once they get in. The grind of pandering and pitting factions against one another never really ends. The mighty beaver bites its own tail, producing fractious minority governments and shifting regional resentments, the simmering sense that somewhere, somehow, another province is getting more goodies from whoever's running Ottawa.

"Big government" is a bogeyman, one deployed by the same people who brought you Homeland Security, among other expansions of intrusive federal power and burdensome public debt. "Big government" is a buzzword, half of a false choice, a hyperbolic contest between totalitarianism and lawlessness, tyranny and liberty. But government isn't Cineplex popcorn: we don't have to choose between way too much and none at all.

Freedom requires some basic infrastructure, some effective governance, to be more than an applause line in a speech. If you're sick, you are living under the tyranny of the body like some lowly forest creature, and there should be health care to free you. If you're dirt poor, you're subject to the tyrannies of market caprice, and there should be welfare and employment insurance to help you get back on your feet and free to shop again. If you're illiterate or ignorant, you are subject to the tyrannies of demagoguery, pseudo-science, and marketing, and there should be daycares, schools, and universities to liberate you, to help you free yourself from the neck up, which is the most important freedom of all.

Rather than insisting that we have intellectual rights and responsibilities, as Enlightenment types like the Founding Fathers did, freedumb – the ideology of idiocracy – consists of two fundamentally contradictory propositions. First, we should do whatever Big Dad says, whether he comes in the form of God or Dick Cheney or Wall Street. But freedumb also tells us that we can do whatever we like, because we're free to ignore those who think they know better. We're free to tell them that they don't know what they're talking about, regardless of what we know. We are all the leading experts on ourselves and our wants, and that is what idiot politics speaks to, addressing millions of private yous instead of a public we.

If you replace the *freedom*s in political speeches with other words such as *safety* or *money,* they acquire a refreshing candour and coherence. Freedom has been trivialized by some of its most vocal enthusiasts, who have successfully rebranded it as freedumb: the right not to give a shit or know jack about what happens, the right to make and support decisions on the grounds of guts and grudges and greed. And with these rights come responsibilities: *Stop whining and get back to work.*

Armies, cops, and fire departments are the only public services that most freedumb fighters support, the only fruits of governance that justify themselves with real benefits. The thin green, blue, and red lines between Homeowner McAverage

and suicide bombers, rapists, and crackheads are the only sac-
rosanct public trust. Right-wingers like Cheney and Harper
talk tough and play bully to remind all of us that we should be
scared shitless and grateful for the protection of our hired
brawn. To ask anything more of the government, to charge it
with tasks other than laissez-faire economic management and
the deployment of force, is churlish, childish, naive at best,
and communist at worst.

In his inaugural address, Obama said:

> What the cynics fail to understand is that the
> ground has shifted beneath them – that the stale
> political arguments that have consumed us for so
> long no longer apply. The question we ask today
> is not whether our government is too big or too
> small, but whether it works . . .

His initial attempts to make government work have been
greeted with howls of protest about the gub'mint takeover of
put-near everything. A Rasmussen poll conducted in February
2009 found that 59 per cent of respondents still agreed with
Reagan: government was the problem, not the solution. A
Gallup poll released in September of that year found that 57
per cent of respondents believed that the government was
doing too much, and 45 per cent said there was too much
government regulation.[28] These numbers are pretty astonish-
ing and depressing, especially when you consider that the
government was doing "too much" because it had to. Private
interests had left it little choice when they screwed the global

economy six ways to Sunday and then importuned government for handouts and help.

Bankers grovelled before the governments they usually revile, like wispy poets whining for grant money. They got billions in bailouts, yet somehow the financial sector still inspires more trust and respect than the government that saved it from itself.

This shows us that the North American public's Stockholm syndrome towards the real elites remains powerful. Freedumb will not, cannot die. The breakdowns and bailouts did not educate or convert the idiocrats. Instead they have become more adamant and entrenched and the war against gub'mint is growing more intemperate and illogical. For a few brief weeks after the financial meltdown started, I thought that maybe this economic crash would mark the end of the idiocracy and show the world how counterproductive anti-government governance is. I must have caught some of that contagious hope that was in the air. Suffice it to say that the weird warm feeling has passed.

Chapter Six

MORE IS LESS

The Media–Entertainment Perplex

———

Flat is the new up.

— RECESSION-BATTERED MEDIA-BIZ CATCHPHRASE

T he media, like Alice in Wonderland, have gotten huge and shrunk, grown bigger and smaller. But the world of media is weirder than Wonderland, since it is growing and shrinking *at the same time.* Old journalism has suffered mass layoffs and speaks to an aging and dwindling audience. But the media in the broad sense – the infoswamp of celebrity gossip, political scandals, fragments of economic data, heinous crimes, lifestyle advice, personal narratives, and just plain weird events – has grown much larger, enveloping North America entire in its miasma, its fog and flickering lights.

There are fewer journalists now than there were before the recession. Tens of thousands of staffers in print, TV, publishing, and radio have been laid off since 2008. At the same time, everyone and her dog can now be a microparticle of the media and say her piece about the issue or scandal *du jour*. Of course, papers have published letters to the editor and radio stations have done call-in shows for ages. But now the audience is moving from commenting to providing content, becoming more integrated into programming, like product placement instead of commercials.

Getting your readers or viewers to write copy or fill airtime is an irresistible combo of populism and cheapness (see also reality TV). You can make the audience do some of the content provision or revision for free rather than overpaying some buncha hacks. Many comment boards on news sites, for example, are full of free copyedits of hastily posted stories. Producers and editors can occupy the idle hours and empty pages of a slow news day by getting the audience to tell them what they think about the latest info crumbs and incitements. This flatters the audience too. It tells them that the average person's opinion is just as good and germane as some journalist's version of the events or some expert's interpretation of a situation. It's similar to the rhetoric of tax cuts: *you know better than we do, so please tell us what to tell you.*

This is also part of a broader social trend. Things that used to be considered jobs or skills have become choices we can make, evidence of market freedom on the march. We are free to scan our own groceries at the self-service checkout, free to be our own bank tellers, free to pump our own gas. We are free to assemble our own furniture and execute our own stock trades. So too are we free to make our own wee bit of the news, be that in the form of a text or message-board post, a cellphone pic of a disaster, a hit YouTube video, or a particularly piquant blog, tweet, or status update.

Even though virtually everyone with access to a computer has unprecedented access to the media and opportunities to opine, the press is still considered part of the hated nerd elite. The media get lumped in with the brains who control everything, slotted somewhere between the diabolical professoriate (smarter and uglier than the media) and well-heeled Hollywood degenerates (stupider and prettier than the media).

At the same time, many nerds think the media are part of the problem. Cultural critics are often quick to blame the media for the decline of this or that venerable noun, to argue that what passes for news dumbs us all down. The right has produced a barge-load of books about liberal media bias, the left has long held that the media are corporate shills, and many retired journalists have written tomes a lot like those university-decline books I mentioned in Chapter Four. Apparently everything was better and truer when reporters typed their own copy piss-drunk while sporting a snazzy hat.

This is simply to say that the media occupy a strange position, insofar as the money-minded think the media are in league with the brains, and vice versa. This is partly the media's own damn fault. The mainstream media's equivocal coverage – stories that ping back and forth between the two sides that every issue is reduced to – provides all the camps with examples of their preferred bias. Moreover, the expanding mediaverse includes more explicitly partisan media organizations, ranging from Fox to MSNBC to the online mags and bloggers on the right and the left.

Media is a small collective noun for a very big part of our landscape, a word that has been stretched as thin and see-through as a wet T-shirt. We demand a lot of a term when we ask it to cover everything from the online chatter on Facebook and Twitter to dead-tree news organs such as the *New York Times* and the *Globe and Mail* to infotainment like TMZ.com, Glenn Beck, and Stephen Colbert.

The sprawl of new blogs, news aggregators, and channels means that audiences have access to news 24-7, and there are sites and shows for nearly every niche interest. Never have people had so many opportunities to learn about the latest developments in weather, the stock market, sports scores, home renovation, or celebrity overdoses. Just as we enjoy unprecedented levels of educational participation, so too do we enjoy more media than ever before. This proliferation, however, does not necessarily produce more news.

Instead, aggregators like Google News, the Drudge Report, and the Huffington Post hork up multiple versions of the same couple of dozen current events every day. Many of these stories are just your local paper's truncation or elaboration of wire copy from one of the big news services such as Reuters, AP, and the Canadian Press; others are barely warmed-over PR releases from one lobby or another. And then those stories drive the cable coverage and become blog fodder. As the nice people from the Project for Excellence in Journalism note, "While the news is always on, there is not a constant flow of new events. The level of repetition in the 24-hour news cycle is one of the most striking features one finds in examining a day of news."[1]

Print may still serve as a primary source of stories that appear on TV and the Web, but that certainly does not help its financial situation. Miasmatic media spread means that more people see snippets of stories floating in the mist of cable channels, late-night comedy shows, talk radio, and Facebook feeds, and thus feel no need to buy the paper. The old media are having a hard time competing with, or adapting to, the speed and low-to-no cost of online content. The top-ranked American newspaper website is the *New York Times* site, according to Internet traffic monitor Alexa.com. Web traffic fluctuates constantly, but the *New York Times* site generally places well behind other info sites such as ESPN and CNN. Canoe.ca, a portal for all the dunderheaded Sun papers, is the top Canadian print-affiliated site, and it usually lags well behind CBC.ca, which trails CNN.com.

The top sites in North America – Google and Facebook – are both good examples of the way the media have gotten huge and global and granular and local at the same time. Google offers access to a goodly chunk of the world's news. It is a ghost library of positively Borgesian proportions, but it is also a librarian that fetches texts based on your preferences. Googling "Obama + awesome" and "Obama + Anti-Christ" produces two different heaps of information from different sources with different spins. Facebook is even more preferential, providing the latest micro-news according to you and your friends: Katie finally pooped in the potty, Jon is tired, Kelly misses Michael Jackson, and Bob reckons he's just as worthy of the Nobel Peace Prize as Obambi.

Google and Facebook are practically infinite. Ditto for Wikipedia, another top-ranked user-generated site. In 2009 an artist named Rob Matthews printed and bound a selection of Wikipedia articles, producing a knee-high five-thousand-page monster. And that volume included only 437 articles plucked from the twenty-five hundred or so "feature" articles that Wikipedia editors deemed the most worthy, the *crème de la* crowd-sourcing floating atop millions of pages of wildly varying quality.

The spread and the specificity of online information have been hell on general-interest organs such as newspapers, *Reader's Digest*, and *Time*, and on niche-ier magazines as well. Plenty of publications died during the economic downturn of 2008–09. Dozens of magazines, ranging from *Cosmo Girl* to *ManDate* to *Gourmet* to *Vibe*, ceased production. Papers that have been in business for over a century, such as the *Rocky Mountain Times*, also closed down.

Others slashed their print runs to survive, such as Canada's *National Post*, which no longer appears on the east coast or on summer Mondays. Some outfits now exist as online-only versions of their former selves, such as the *Seattle Post-Intelligencer* and the *Christian Science Monitor,* and the *New York Times* had to mortgage its posh new digs and scrounge a loan from Mexican billionaire Carlos Slim Helu. Hell, even *USA Today*, the paper for the massiest of masses, has suffered a dip in its circulation rates.

All that bad news meant that newspaper stocks tanked too. A graph of print-media company share prices throughout the recession shows a steep drop-off, a plunge down a sheer rocky slope. (If you fell down it, your injuries would definitely net you a few lines of concerned local coverage.) In 2009 Democratic congressman Benjamin Cardin proposed that imperilled American newspapers get some federal assistance. He did not propose anything so radical as a pile of bailout cash or free subscriptions for eighteen-year-olds like that commie frog Sarkozy's 600-million-euro press rescue package (roughly 890 to 930 billion U.S. or Canadian dollars, depending on exchange rates). Cardin's Newspaper Revitalization Act proposes reclassifying ailing newspapers as non-profits; then they could reap the resulting tax breaks and the papers would be more like PBS than TMZ.

Obama said he was open to this proposal in an interview in September 2009, but he was speaking to a newspaper, the *Toledo Blade*. The right promptly and loudly denounced the proposal as yet more federal meddling in the free market, another costly nationalization of a failed business model that was too liberal to live. Moreover, the right also alleged that any government assistance for print media would represent the total propagandization of an already grossly over Obamafied nation. *Bad enough that he's the star of the news; he sure as shit shouldn't be the boss of it too.*

Youngish pundits and tech junkies also scoffed at the prospect of a print media bailout. They said this move made about as much sense as giving GM money to keep on cranking out gas-guzzling dinomobiles nobody wants. Whatever happened to the cleansing powers of creative destruction? Those big, dumb, lumbering papers should have seen the Internet coming and erected pay walls around their content sometime in the 1990s. Or newspapers could have adopted some kind of micropayment structure to monetize their sites. They could have, should have done something – anything really – but play dodo and deny the inevitable.

Cheerleaders for online news claim it can do the same work as print media, and do it quicker and slicker, cleaner and greener, leaner and meaner. Bemoaning the fate of bloated old institutions like the Gray Lady is a waste of time, they say, a wallow in nostalgia that mistakes the paper for the news and ignores the way new media might revitalize journalism. The real challenge is finding new ways to fund old-fangled journalistic endeavours such as investigative reporting, local beats, and political coverage, which are not as ad-friendly or lucrative, on or offline, as lifestyle fluff, gossip, and sports. Who will furnish those who watch the watchmen with coffee, doughnuts, and broadband? Noble philanthropic foundations? Righteous indie collectives? Members-only subscriptions? Or will they be lone wolves, living off their wits and clicks?

Nobody knows yet. Consequently, the death-of-journalism meme is getting even more play than the end of the Enlightenment. It too is a bipartisan declinism. In 2009, in his capacity as a commentator for Fox News, Mike Huckabee delivered an obituary for "a good friend to all of us" – journalism. He alleged that the profession had died of acute head injuries incurred by tripping all over itself to serve the beloved Obama.[2] The notion that the media are part of the necrotic, tottering elite has long been a favourite Fox News theme, one that allows the channel to present itself not as part of the media, but as the voice of the people, the brave new populist alternative to rotten old reportage. Jigging on journalism's grave is Huckabee, Hannity, and Beck's job.

However, lefty news sites such as Alternet, Daily Kos, and Rabble.ca make the same case, arguing that they represent a genuinely populist alternative to the corrupt and compromised lapdog press. These sites allege that Fox is just the most enthusiastic and egregious gang of media whores turning tricks for military and corporate power. Their rhetoric also displays contempt for the stooges in the mainstream media. A truly liberal or lefty media would neither have corroborated nor complaisantly communicated the Bush administration's secrets and lies about Iraq's putative WMDs, domestic surveillance, or torture. Stories like Abu Ghraib broke online first because old journalism was too cowed and compliant, too worried about losing its access to power, to handle the ugly truth.

Partisan media outlets sell themselves as the anti-media and the actual media. Like an anti-government pol on the campaign trail, they see the problem and are the solution. It's the same pitch – this is the *real* real – regardless of their size or their side. Glenn Beck and Sean Hannity are part of the lucrative Murdoch empire, while their lefty equivalents customarily rely on the kindness of strangers and Kashi ads. Meanwhile, the traditional media encourage and exploit both camps, plucking provocative material from them and mashing up their positions, creating a muddle that is supposed to represent the sensible middle.

This attempted bipartisanship does not seem to be working. A majority of Americans still think the media are liberal, and a vocal minority of them want them to die for that very reason. Then there are the up-with-tech types who want newspapers to die because they are old. Whether they skew liberal or libertarian, hippyish or addled by Ayn Rand, these techies treat the death of newspapers as a renaissance of journalism and democracy. If the old media must die to make way for the thousands of infoblossoms blooming online, so be it. The grandpa media missed the biggest *Extra! Extra!* of all, the one about their own impending superfluity and obsolescence: most people under thirty-five ambled over to *The Daily Show* and the Web to meet their news needs years ago. Newspapers are like unto typewriters and rotary phones to them.

Losing the youth is an obvious sign that old news media are getting smaller. But the news is also shrinking *because* it is growing. More news outlets means a smaller audience share for any single paper, network, or website. While all three might dog-pile on similar stories and parrot a lot of wire copy, they also put a particular spin on their delivery and selection of that material. In the same way that the buffet of charter schools undermines the notion of schools as social glue, media proliferation undermines the idea of the press as a public institution or source of common knowledge. Instead, the veracity of any media outlet becomes a matter of private taste. There is news for you and people like you; then there are the channels and blogs that you and yours will never patronize, unless you are trawling for yuks and wrongness.

Some have argued that this is part of the reason why political discourse remains so polarized, in spite of all the polls claiming that people want their representatives to quit bickering, in spite of Obama's many "there are no red states, no blue states, only the United States" speeches. As Texan journalist Bill Bishop explains in his 2008 book, *The Big Sort,* Americans live in increasingly ideologically homogeneous communities, landslide districts of either Republicans or Democrats. They also consume media that cater to their particular political world view. Bishop sums it up succinctly in his Big Sort blog on Slate.com: "We read apart, live apart, watch apart, blog apart, and drive apart; we are one country that lacks any shared experiences or, it seems, common purpose."[3]

Bishop argues that there is an echo-chamber effect at work here too. When like minds flock together in a specific burb or on a particular corporate, editorial, or web board, people distinguish themselves by adopting increasingly extreme versions of the group's consensus opinions. This is one of the reasons why the anti-war and anti-trade side and the anti-gub'mint side both compare the president to Hitler, even though they paint their little moustaches on different presidents. This helps explain why a recent poll, conducted by Sacred Heart University, found that Fox News was simultaneously the most and least trusted news source: 30 per cent of the respondents said it was the most reliable network and 26 per cent ranked it dead last.[4]

Newspapers have always run partisan, sensational, or scandalous material. That's not new. What has changed is that the media have broken down the barrier that formerly separated entertainment and news, so we consume facts and events the same way we consume fun: according to our personal preferences. It is pointless to pine for a simpler time like the three-channels-and-two-local-papers age, when almost everyone trusted Walter Cronkite.

When Cronkite shuffled off this mortal coil in 2009, many journalists and media critics covered his death as another obituary for journalism. He had been retired since the early eighties, but his former colleagues turned his death into a symbol of the end of serious news, the kind that used to inspire trust and sway public opinion and politics.

The fragmentation and multiplication of the media mean that participants in public policy arguments, such as the debate about health care, bring very different sets of facts and interpretations to the table, ones that are often incommensurable. Talking heads are unlikely to find any sort of sensible middle or reasonable compromise between "We need a public option" and "This is socialist tyranny."

It is disingenuous for news organizations to claim that they seek balance or neutrality when they get some blogger who hates Obama to go head-to-head with a Democratic operative. What they really want, what their questions provoke, is a fight – the drama, emotion, and snaps of clashing camps skirmishing. The news is just a wonkier version of the same stuff that sells in other branches of the entertainment industry: conflict between characters. The difference between a UFC bout, Kanye West vs. the world, and a spat between opposing members of Congress or Parliament is increasingly one of degree rather than kind.

News organizations, like other branches of the entertainment industry, pimp themselves with promotional merch. Coffee mugs and tote bags are as old as Pledge Week, but

the Fox News store also offers fifteen different ties, golf par-
aphernalia, books by a number of its on-air personalities,
and a branded watch. The CNN store sells T-shirts emblazoned with your favourite infotaining headline. Popular
choices include "Obama Beats McCain" and "1 in 3 Workers
Hungover at Office." Under the banner of "offbeat," one can
purchase "Poop Power Saves City Money" and "Pole Dance
Ends with Face Plant."

Journalism even has its own combination theme park
and mausoleum. In 2008 the Newseum, a $450 million facil-
ity years in the making, finally opened. Previously housed in
much more modest digs in Rosslyn, Virginia, the Newseum
now occupies a massive, splashy building in Washington,
D.C., down the road from the Capitol. It hosts a collection of
journalism artifacts, interactive displays, multiple movie theatres playing video clips, a working production studio, trib-
utes to journalists who have died in the line of duty, a gift
shop, a food court, and a more upscale Wolfgang Puck eatery.

The millions of bucks that built the Newseum came from
people who own newspapers, like the Gannetts (*USA Today*)
and the Sulzbergers (the *New York Times*). The news industry
is trying to burnish its image by presenting its own infotaining version of journalism's history and future. Like the
Creation Museum, the Newseum borrows some gravitas from
museology and history to make its case, then wraps all that
serious info and old jive in fun for the whole family, in entertaining flicks and interactive displays.

It's very difficult to disentangle news and entertainment
when the news is trying to save itself by borrowing the

trappings of entertainment. But news organizations are also turning to entertainment for cheap content as the traditional media piggyback on celebrity gossip sites and blogs. TMZ, a Time Warner tentacle that started online in 2005, has broken several big stories that eventually ended up gobbling plenty of mainstream airtime and inches of op-ed angst. Notable examples include Mel Gibson's arrest and anti-Semitic outburst, Kramer's krazy racist Komedy Klub meltdown, and Michael Jackson's death.

TMZ has been criticized for its sensationalism and the creepy insistence of its paparazzi. Critics allege that its editors pay sources and use less stringent standards than the traditional media, but TMZ gets many stories the old-fashioned way, by sifting through documents, working sources in hospitals, police departments, and restaurants, and pestering the ever-living shit out of its targets.

This is simply to say that TMZ is an odd blend of old and new media, of traditional gumshoe reportage, the immediacy of the Web, and the superficiality of celebrity culture. When TMZ beat the *L.A. Times* to the story of Michael Jackson's death, some saw this scoop as the new media triumphing over the moribund old press. Others refused to acknowledge TMZ as a legit source. CNN journos, for example, waffled about announcing Jackson's death until the *L.A. Times* did. They mentioned that TMZ was claiming Jackson was dead, but Wolf Blitzer insisted that they wait for more confirmation. They might be corporate cousins – CNN also belongs to Time Warner – but CNN seemed wary of TMZ, as if it couldn't quite trust the louche online upstart.

This old-media hauteur is funny when you think about how much time CNN anchors spend reading viewer tweets and emails, deploying whiz-bang techno props like digital maps and holograms, and covering the same celebrities as TMZ.

In a 2007 article in the *New York Times,* Harvey Levin, the legalist and investigative reporter who is the Grand Poo-Bah of TMZ, compared it to the Associated Press. He said, "We work as hard at breaking a Britney Spears story as NBC would work on breaking a President Bush piece."[5] If Levin and his bevy of youngsters had dogged Bush and Cheney in the lead-up to the Iraq war with the same tenacity that they monitor Lindsay Lohan's leatheriness, perhaps some of their scandals might have broken sooner.

Sure, TMZ covers vapid dingbats, but it does not worship them. It treats them much more harshly than the publicist-approved puff pieces we see on *etalk* or in the likes of *Vanity Fair*. It is a lot less deferential than the Hollywood or Washington press corps. Much of TMZ's coverage is mean, smirky, and snarky, more likely to bury Paris Hilton than to praise her.

It's easy to point to TMZ as yet another example of our brainless celebrity culture. Celeb gossip clogs the airwaves and Intertubes, crowding out more important stories. Rich, dizzy babes of questionable talent are bad role models for the kids. It's a shame that pantyless party girls get more attention than the real heroes, the nurses and teachers and moms. All true, my earnest friend, all true. But that doesn't really explain why people like TMZ. Loving gossip is certainly part of it, but TMZ also caters to our seemingly endless appetite for bad examples, stupid statements, and morons to mock.

Talentless stars and clueless celebs are not really role models, at least not to the extent that some parents and cultural critics fear they are. Rather, the coverage of these stars tends to range from the faux concerned to the downright derisive. Celebrities often serve as objects of *schadenfreude,* a way for the audience to make fun of dummies and congratulate themselves for being more sensible or smarter than the rich and powerful. Britney or Heidi and Spencer might have money, fame, and miles of shoes, but they are miserable or moronic or dopey or douchey.

Laughing at the clueless mouthfarts of cute twenty-somethings who spent their high-school years with vocal coaches or plastic surgeons is another variation on the theme "Are we getting dumber?" Ignorant or loopy celebs allow the public to express and exorcise their own anxieties about their intelligence. *Jesus Christ, are all young people this stunned? Why is this trash in the paper? Who likes these people?* Celebrity stories also offer a chance to complain about the whims of the free market. The economic excesses of celebrities always make for good gossip. *Ten million bucks to get* her *in your movie? He's bankrupt because he blew it all on jewellery and tigers?*

The publicly and lavishly squandered fortunes of celebrities – TMZ shoots a lot of shopping footage – tell us that economic rewards are fickle, fleeting, dependent only on popularity. Sometimes talent and hard work are rewarded and sometimes the world's Kardashians prevail. One day everyone loves you, execs are hucking millions at you, and you're buying mink-lined Uggs for all your pals, who chill at your mansion. Next thing you know, you're outta work, in hock, and scrambling for a spot on *Celebrity Rehab.*

Like school-sucks stories or accounts of campus decline, celeb coverage allows the media to play on our anxieties about how ignorant our fellows are, or are becoming. Then there are the semi-celebs who enjoy brief fame for blurting or doing something stupid, making a mistake egregious enough for the vast majority to point and laugh at. The most infamous recent example of this occurred in August 2007, when Miss Teen USA contestant Lauren Caitlin Upton served up this word salad:

> I personally believe that U.S. Americans are unable to [locate the U.S. on a map] because, uh, some, people out there in our nation don't have maps and, uh, I believe that our, uh, education like such as, uh, South Africa and, uh, the Iraq, everywhere like such as, and, I believe that they should, our education over here in the U.S. should help the U.S., uh, or, uh, should help South Africa and should help the Iraq and the Asian countries, so we will be able to build up our future, for our children.

The clip became a popular news item and an instant smash on YouTube, where it racked up millions and millions of hits and thousands and thousands of comments.

Upton quickly parlayed this exposure into follow-up appearances on programs such as the *Today Show,* where she was given an opportunity to answer the question again. She said:

> Personally, my friends and I, we know exactly where the United States is on a map. I don't know anyone else who doesn't. If the statistics are correct, I believe there should be more emphasis on geography in our education so people will learn how to read maps better.[6]

The hosts applauded her for this effort, which is not much of an improvement on the original. The grammar is better, insofar as there is some. But it is still redundant and narcissistic, disputing the stats on the grounds of her finger's-breadth of experience, making an *argumentum ad* I-don't-know-anyone-like-that, a popular undergrad essay move.

Upton may have lost the pageant but she won the publicity, became part of the media mist. (Can you remember who won? Me neither.) Her garble was second only to "Don't tase me, bro!" in the *Yale Dictionary of Quotations* list of 2007's most notable quotes. NBC, the network that broadcast the pageant, also used Upton's jibber-jabber to promote the pageant in 2008. Their pitch: *Come see which one of these dizzy babes will lose her cool and say something ridiculous this year.*

Upton got her fifteen minutes because she is a blonde-joke blonde who gave America the opportunity to ask itself the question "Does this bonehead represent an endemic national boneheadedness?" The morning shows answered this with a resounding no. *She's just a pretty girl who cracked under the pressure – time for a makeup test and a cookie!* The Web is a much harsher taskmaster. Bloggers and posters reviled Upton for embodying a host of bobble-head stereotypes of ladies and blondes and Americans. The general tone? *Thanks a lot, you ditzy bitch, for handing the world's lesser nations yet another chance to point and jeer at that big ol' doofus the U.S. of A.*

There is a lot of wrong on the Internet: page after page of execrable grammar, bad information, and delusional ranting. But it also hosts countless sites devoted to the excoriation of ignorance and sloppiness, where the persnickety share and shred everything from poorly spelled signs to disingenuous reporting. The Internet is also home to various experts – professors, economists, statisticians, veterans of the old press – who can provide more detailed interpretations of ongoing events than the confines and constraints of a column or cable squabble allow.

A 2009 survey by the Pew Research Center for People and the Press found that more people were getting their national and international news from the Internet than from newspapers. Forty-two per cent of respondents went to the Net for news and 33 per cent still trusted ol' Inky. But the vast majority, 71 per cent, said that TV was their primary news source. This helps explain another finding from the survey: the accuracy and credibility of the press has tanked. Pew has been conducting this survey for nearly two decades. In 2009 the number of respondents who said that the press usually gets things right, 29 per cent, sank to its all-time low. The majority, 63 per cent, said news stories were often inaccurate, and 60 per cent thought the news was politically biased.[7]

Republicans have been working this angle since the 1980s, arguing that bland moderate media outlets like CNN, which frequently air the opinions of corporate lobbyists, are actually radical leftist organs. But Democrats increasingly also see the news as biased. Both sides think the press is in cahoots with the powerful people and institutions it should be policing. Both have decamped to their own cable channels. Republicans watch Fox, Democrats watch MSNBC and CNN, and never the twain shall meet.

Though they may put a partisan spin on the events of the day, cable networks and the stodgy old broadcast news organizations share one trait. They chase the latest blip, no matter how trivial or half-baked it may be. The best recent example of this happened on October 15, 2009, when the media entire went apeshit over "Balloon Boy." The story, which was *the* story everywhere that afternoon, went like this: Six-year-old Falcon Heene of Fort Collins, Colorado, climbed into his dad's homemade helium balloon, which somehow managed to get off the ground. The boy was trapped in the unforgiving skies, skidding through the air with helicopters, rescue services, and hordes of reporters in hot pursuit. Where and when would he land? Would he live?

I freely admit that I know very little about physics. But I, like most festivity-attending North Americans, have held a helium balloon. I have also seen balloons fly and float, and Heene's UFOish silver handiwork did not appear to be dragging ballast, or at least not kid-sized ballast. By late afternoon, when the balloon landed, boyless, the media began changing their tack, but nobody dared insinuate it might be a hoax until the next morning, after the family's interview with CNN's Larry King. The boy blurted the wrong thing to the World's Oldest Interviewer, confessing that he'd hidden in a box "for the show."

For the next couple of days, the unravelling hoax led the news. The Heenes were the number-one search topic on Google and the family appeared on ABC and NBC, where the kids were nervous to the point of puking. Reports surfaced that Heene and his wife were long-time publicity hounds and wackadoodle ones at that, who had appeared on ABC's *Wife Swap*. Heene *père* also believes in the Lizard People and chases storms. He concocted the hoax because he was mad with cockamamie dreams of his very own reality show.

The media granted Heene's wish. Media critics saw the Balloon Boy debacle as proof that the press is more interested in being fast than in being right. Just like Web commenters who love to declare "firsties," so too does the boob-tube brigade break stories before they have the relevant details, piling onto the new new thing, fearing that another channel might beat them to a scoop. The result? Hours of repetition, speculation, and vamping as the info trickles in. This torpor is punctuated by occasional feeding frenzies whenever a particularly meaty chunk of info bobs up among the chum. And other stories – the ones scheduled before the latest Shocking Developments! – get bumped. The economy, health care, and Afghanistan can wait until everyone's done gawping at the drifting balloon.

Again, as in the Lauren Upton example, the Internet media were much harsher in their assessment of the story than the mainstream. Bloggers and message-board posters argued that the story was likely a hoax while the balloon was still in the air. Of course, it is easier to speculate about a child's life from behind the Web's veil of anonymity. At the same time, I saw a lot more balloon-related physics online than I did on CNN, and bloggers were quick to link to old YouTube clips of Papa Heene having conniptions on *Wife Swap*.

Once it became clear that the story was indeed a hoax, the old media lingered in Fort Collins for well over a week, providing constant updates about the likelihood of Heene's being charged or fined for his shenanigans. Sheriff Jim Alderden told reporters, "I am confident that you folks have something better to do."[8] The next day, Alderden appeared on Fox's *O'Reilly Report*.

Like bad dinner guests, TV reporters show up too early and stay too late. They rush stories to air, throwing what little they know at the audience to see what sticks. If a story attracts a lot of attention, they flog it until the audience starts to turn on the tale. Then they dump it down the memory hole, never to be seen again. Internet time is different; stories appear online even more rapidly than they do on TV, and they linger longer too. The Internet allows people to participate in the story, to embroider it with their opinions or expertise in ways TV does not. Granted, sometimes this degenerates into commentary that is the digital equivalent of dirty graffiti in a bathroom stall, but there is also a lot of really great, thoughtful writing on the Web.

Some have gone so far as to claim that this is a golden age of writing. In *The Economist*'s More Intelligent Life blog, professor Anne Trubek declared in June 2009 that "we are all writers now."⁹ Her students' steady diet of Facebook status updates, texts, emails, and tweets meant they were reading and writing more than previous generations. A similar article in *Wired* two months later showcased the work of professor Andrea Lunsford, whose study of Stanford students' writing habits found that they were doing more and more "life-writing" outside the classroom. "I think we're in the midst of a literacy revolution the likes of which we haven't seen since Greek civilization," she said.¹⁰

It is indeed true that young people are typing more than their forebears. But that has not led to any marked improvements in the student essays and emails I've seen over the past decade. I haven't done a formal study, but the thousands of pages I've corrected strongly suggest the following: Students who read books, for class and for fun, write fairly well in class and online. Students who balk at reading books send me mangled, misspelled emails and hand in essays that drain my marking pens.

This optimism about the transformative powers of the Internet becomes a problem when it starts to affect the education system. The idea that schools and universities should abandon books and follow the kids online, meeting them where their cool new literacies live, is wrong. If students are going to spend more time writing and reading, they need a rigorous education more than ever, to serve as a counterweight to the speedy, sometimes sloppy and slapdash nature of the Net.

I love the Web. However, I do not think, like some tech-noptimists, that skimming blogs or completing a Facebook quiz is equivalent to reading challenging material and learning how to make an argument about it. Rather, unprecedented access to information means it is all the more urgent that we teach students how to evaluate that information, how to judge the countless claims on sites of wildly varying quality.

Print culture and digital culture may overlap, but there are still significant differences between them. Perhaps the starkest example of the difference is the Modern Library's list of the top one hundred English-language novels of the twentieth century. The editors posted their choices and then encouraged Web-types to vote for their favourites. The editors' top ten selections were

1. *Ulysses* (James Joyce)
2. *The Great Gatsby* (F. Scott Fitzgerald)
3. *A Portrait of the Artist as a Young Man* (James Joyce)
4. *Lolita* (Vladimir Nabokov)
5. *Brave New World* (Aldous Huxley)
6. *The Sound and the Fury* (William Faulkner)
7. *Catch-22* (Joseph Heller)
8. *Darkness at Noon* (Arthur Koestler)
9. *Sons and Lovers* (D. H. Lawrence)
10. *The Grapes of Wrath* (John Steinbeck)

I think *Lolita* is better than *Gatsby* or *Portrait,* but this is a pretty predictable canonical ranking. Hundreds of thousands of Internet voters produced the following list:

1. *Atlas Shrugged* (Ayn Rand)
2. *The Fountainhead* (Ayn Rand)
3. *Battlefield Earth* (L. Ron Hubbard)
4. *The Lord of the Rings* (J. R. R. Tolkien)
5. *To Kill a Mockingbird* (Harper Lee)
6. *1984* (George Orwell)
7. *Anthem* (Ayn Rand)
8. *We the Living* (Ayn Rand)
9. *Mission Earth* (L. Ron Hubbard)
10. *Fear* (L. Ron Hubbard)

This poll ran in 1998, when publishers were just starting to dabble in digital democracy. The Modern Library launched the project to get people talking about the great books, and hundreds of thousands of people did. Lamentably, the majority flipped the bird at the great books and mass-clicked in support of agitprop for objectivism and Scientology, two of the twentieth century's daffiest dogmas.[11]

I imagine this list might look slightly different now. Ayn's turgid, rapey doorstops would still do well, but she and L. Ron might have to cede a couple of slots to recent blockbusters like the *Left Behind* books and the *Twilight* franchise. These books have some of the highest scores and the most ardent fans, so they must be the greatest. Conversely, nobody really likes – or reads – challenging shit like *Ulysses*. And any nerds who say that they do are likely indulging in old-culture snobbery, affecting cultural preferences to make other people feel dumb.

The death-of-book-reading story has been getting a fair amount of play in the press, since it goes beautifully with the demise of journalism. For example, when a reporter from the *New York Times* asked Apple's Steve Jobs in early 2008 about plans for an iNifty e-book reader, he dismissed the idea outright: "It doesn't matter how good or bad the product is, the fact is that people don't read anymore. Forty per cent of the people in the U.S. read one book or less last year. The whole conception is flawed at the top because people don't read anymore."[12]

The National Endowment for the Arts has tracked the number of Americans who read for pleasure since the 1980s, and their reports have consistently shown that fewer Americans, particularly young Americans, read books. But their most recent survey, released in 2008, revealed a nice little jump: a 7 per cent increase in the number of adults who read. More young people were picking up books too. The number of eighteen-to-twenty-four-year-olds who read had increased by 9 per cent.

This is happy news, but the NEA survey doesn't tell us what people are reading, beyond broad categories like poetry and drama (down) or novels and short stories (up). Those increases could represent the combined effects of *Harry Potter*, *Twilight*, and unemployment. Reading is cheap, recession-friendly fun. And even though the number of readers is growing, the U.S. remains pretty evenly split on reading: 50.2 per cent of the respondents had read a novel in the past year; 54 per cent had read a book – any book – without their school or employer forcing them to do so.[13]

Canadians fancy themselves more bookish than the neighbours, but this depends on whom you ask. A 2007 poll, conducted by Ipsos-Reid for CanWest Global, found that fewer Canadians than Americans read: 31 per cent of respondents had not read a single book that year.[14] A 2007 report on the retail book trade, published by Canadian Heritage, was much more positive, asserting that the number of Canucks who read for pleasure stayed consistent throughout the 1990s and 2000s. However, based on StatsCan numbers from 2005, they also claim that nine out of ten Canadians read for pleasure, which frankly seems way too good to be true.[15]

Again, like the NEA surveys, this doesn't tell us much about what people are reading. A cursory scan of the fiction and non-fiction bestseller lists on either side of the border reveals that most North Americans like the same things: vampires, magic, spirituality, conspiracies, celebrities, weight loss, getting rich quick, and triumphing over adversity.

One of the biggest bestsellers on both sides of the border lo these past few years is Randy Pausch's *The Last Lecture*. Like many publishing sensations, it started as something else, achieving success in another cultural medium before it became a book. Pausch delivered the lecture in 2007 at his home campus, Carnegie Mellon University, where he taught computer programming. He had recently learned that he had pancreatic cancer, and he used the speech to deliver life lessons to his very young children. The speech became a hit on YouTube, Pausch appeared on Oprah, and the lecture appeared in book form in the spring of 2008.

Pausch's book enjoyed a seventy-nine-week ride on the *New York Times* advice list, and it was on the *Globe and Mail*'s non-fiction bestseller list for more than a year. This is the kind of book that people buy in triplicate, quadruplicate, to give to their friends and relatives. It was a smash, but it did not manage to best Mitch Albom's 205-week streak of NYT bestsellerdom for *Tuesdays with Morrie,* another sentimental swan song from a wise prof. Pausch, to be fair, joked about the success of both books. "I didn't know there was a dying professor section at the bookstore," he said.[16]

If there were a dying professor section, it would do much brisker trade than one dedicated to the work of vigorous nerds. Suffering the inevitable, suffering cheerfully and gratefully, is a far more impressive credential than any degree. Even people who gave Pausch's book a one-star rating on Amazon prefaced their reviews by saying they were sorry he was dying, they hated to pick on a guy with cancer, but he really shoulda saved this pile of platitudes for his family.

A video of *The Last Lecture* has also aired repeatedly on PBS, where a pledge-week host enthused, "Did you notice that Randy uses the word *dream* more than the words *teach* or *learn?*" I did – it's hard not to – but I was considerably less tickled by that than the talking head was. Pausch offers a very contemporary cocktail of techno-rationalism and sentiment. His title for the lecture was "Really Achieving Your Childhood Dreams," and he talks about how he did precisely that, by never giving up, by greeting every brick wall as a new opportunity. Pausch is also part of Camp Quit Bitching. One of his chapter titles is "Don't Complain, Just Work Harder," the kind of jocular, boss-friendly advice that is common in positive thinking.

Pausch mocks the professoriate, telling us that he's always

felt uncomfortable in academia, as "he comes from a long line of people who had to work for a living." He repeatedly says that his unique practical, technical master's degree could not happen at any old conventional university, and sneers at the merely theoretical. For example, when his students arrive, he tells them, "No more book-learning. You've already spent four years doing book-learning." Instead his students get to consort with Pixar and make "real" projects such as artificial computer environments and simulations.

Pausch is the ideal professor for a culture that does not like professors very much. He taught computer programming, and anything related to computers is a serious major, a lucrative major, the "one word: plastics" of the twenty-first century. However, he does not spend much time talking about his area of expertise, which would doubtless baffle and bore the audience. Instead he tells them things they already know or things they want to believe, such as that hard work will be rewarded and dreams will come true. The lecture is a dying declaration, the farewell of a good dad and husband with an especially evil disease, which appeals to our taste for the maudlin and the morbid. But his jokey demeanour also demonstrates the pluck-in-the-face-of-adversity that positive thinkers adore.

The educational computer program Pausch mentions in the lecture is called Alice, and it is based on Lewis Carroll's *Alice's Adventures in Wonderland.* Pausch and his colleagues may have the technical skills to write a sleek program for a blinky box and make a child's dream come to life on a screen, but when they need ideas – content such as plot or character

– they often end up going back to the mouldy old books. This is also why approximately one-third of all video games take place in the fake Middle Ages. Just as the blogosphere and cable news still leech off newspapers, so too do games, TV shows, and movies feed off the old print culture, for all that they may belittle it or claim to have bested it.

Undaunted by reports of their demise, publishers continue to churn out a mind-boggling number of books. In 2008, U.S. publishers put out over half a million titles. Old-school publishers released 275,232 titles, and even more titles – 285,394 – were available as online print-on-demand books or feats of self-publishing.[17] People have more things to not-read than ever!

The Internet may be growing rapidly, but TV still remains the central hub of the entertainment-media perplex as the medium that promotes books, websites, and movies to the broadest audience. Television displays the same wild variations in quality that the Internet does. Some critics claim that this is a golden age of television, pointing to shows such as *The Wire*, *Deadwood*, and *Mad Men*. Having grown up on total dreck like *Three's Company*, I'm inclined to agree with them.

At the same time, the old-media complexity of these boutique cable programs – critics call them "novelistic" – also shows us how jejune a lot of mainstream TV is. The writer's strike of 2007–08 was a telling moment. Television could keep on trucking for four months, with minimal interruptions, with a skeleton crew scripting it. Who needs writers? People are perfectly happy to watch talent shows, dance contests, and casts of nobodies scheming and squabbling.

Like the Internet, reality TV is a great leveller, an agent of the cultural duh-mocracy that we have in lieu of democratic freedom. Reality TV has also started offering and broadcasting the sorts of social services that used to be the province of the loathed nanny state, such as rebuilding wrecked houses and helping folks lose weight and kick drugs. A&E now features three therapeutic reality shows: *Intervention, Hoarders,* and *Obsessed.* The network has not specialized in Artsy Entertainment for quite some time; the A now stands for autopsies and addictions, and the E is for eating disorders and evading arrest.

Similarly, the Learning Channel schools viewers about ginormous families, life as a little person, and the perils of extreme obesity and undetected pregnancies. The sheer volume of medical programming on TV makes it clear that Americans are anxious about their health and the looming threat of disease and debt. Whether it is in the form of cut-rate re-enactments of procedures gone horribly awry, splashy prime-time dramas about hot doctors, or kindly clinicians like Oprah's pal Dr. Oz telling us what we should eat and how our effluvia should look, health is a constant obsession on TV, almost as ubiquitous as crime.

The most popular drama in Canada, and one of the biggest recent hits in the U.S., is a medical show, one that incorporates the mystery element of crime shows. *House M.D.* features a smart person who embodies some of the nerd stereotypes I listed in the first chapter. His superior mind alienates him from others. He is coldly rational to the point of cruelty, but he also teeters between genius and insanity like a mad scientist or nutty professor. He is lazy and bossy, arrogant and immature. He sucks at life, but he is also preternaturally smart and successful.

House's brains are good because his brilliance is channelled into something useful. It's okay for doctors to be egomaniacal, sarcastic dicks, angry drunk on their own nerdy powers, as long as they save people's lives. Medical dramas and forensic crime shows are also examples of our love of technical reason, our fondness for amazing innovations such as full-body scans and experimental procedures, or those fantastic fictitious machines and computer programs that do most of the thinking on the various CSIs.

House appeals to our love of the spiritual and the sentimental too. Upstanding types like Cameron and Wilson soften House's most destructive intellectual impulses, his corrosive skepticism. House is one of most skeptical characters on network TV, but his discoveries are usually epiphanic, almost mystical, despite his oft-stated allegiance to reason. In most episodes the reasoning process of the differential diagnosis fails, repeatedly, and then the answer arrives as a revelation. Wilson or Cuddy says something seemingly unrelated that sets off a spontaneous brainwave, House snaps to attention, and the mystery is solved.

House's blend of technology and spirituality is very *au courant*. But the real genius of the show is the way that House pleases two very different audiences. Hugh Laurie is a Cambridge-educated British wit (highbrow) whose character speaks perfect American, peppers his rants with slang, and amuses himself with video games and electric guitars (lowbrow). Nerds like yours truly can enjoy the spectacle of a smart man exercising his intellect unfettered by social convention. An intelligent person who requires serious drugs to endure the indignities of a world full of idiots – stupidity pains him as much as his bad leg – is catnip for persecuted nerds. At the same time, the fact that House is a sad, funny monster, a jerk and a junkie, means he also appeals to an anti-intellectual audience by confirming their opinions about the instability, irresponsibility, and godless misery of the nerd elite.

This cultural double-jointedness is one of the reasons why Fox is so successful. Former Fox Entertainment chairman Peter Liguori said, "We're the populist network. The audience always comes first."[18] Fox sells pseudo-populism, but it also pushes products that satirize its pseudo-populist base. The audience comprises at least two groups. One is the dum dums who want to watch cars crash, animals attack, and Paris Hilton attempt to live simply and befriend humans. The other is people who want to laugh at the dum dums who watch that tripe. A really populist network caters to both, so Fox offers products for both self-declared populists (Fox News; their reality roster) and the people who disdain pseudo-populist philistinism (two shows, *Dollhouse* and *Firefly*, by smarty-pants *Buffy* scribe Joss Whedon; *Arrested Development*; the golden age of *The Simpsons*).

Are You Smarter Than a 5th Grader? premiered in February 2007 as one of Fox's best-rated debuts. The show's format has since migrated to other lands, including Canada. Watching adults flub grade-school questions is evidently a global taste. The show revels in taking grown-ups down a peg and salutes the superior intellect of children – a common sentimental myth. It also reproaches those who think they are so smart. The glee when they finally shanghaied the proverbial rocket scientist as a contestant was downright palpable.

A 2007 episode featured *American Idol* contestant Kellie Pickler. She got a grade 3 geography question: Budapest is the capital of what country? She was stumped, and replied, "This might be a stupid question . . . I thought Europe was a country? Budapest? I've never heard of that. I know they speak French there. Is France a country?" There was some banter with the host, redneck comedian Jeff Foxworthy, as he tried to get Pickler to focus, and she responded, "I'm listening to what you're saying but I only hear what I want to," which led to some jolly sexist ribbing. When Pickler heard the right answer (Hungary), she was surprised. "That's a country? I've heard of Turkey . . ."[19] They did manage to confirm at some point in this chucklefest that France is actually a country, where people do speak French, but that Yerp is not.

A few months before *5th Grader* became a big hit, another branch of the Fox media conglomerate released Mike Judge's movie *Idiocracy.* Both have the same theme: people are getting more ignorant and do not know as much as they used to. But *5th Grader* gives ignorance an affectionate pat on the head, treats it like a joke, and waves it away with the healing wisdom of adorable moppets. Conversely, *Idiocracy* is pessimistic and dysgenic. The children, and their children, and their children's children just get dumber and dumber.

Set in the year 2505, when everyone has devolved into a dolt, *Idiocracy* features greedy, grunting, gullible slobs wandering the dirty, decrepit, drought-ridden world that ignorance has built. When the army put Private Joe Bowers, the protagonist, to sleep in 2005, he was utterly average. When he wakes up in the future, he is the smartest man in the world.

Idiocracy is not a great movie. It, like many comedy flicks, is a bit broad and crude, and it eventually succumbs to sap. But it does have some very sharp, funny moments. It jabs reality TV – *Ow, My Balls!* is a hit show – corporate culture, and the movie industry itself. The Oscar-winning *Ass,* a snippet of film within the film, is exactly what it sounds like. *Idiocracy* also mocks the degradation of the English language. For example, a clinician named Doctor Lexus diagnoses Joe thus:

> Don't wanna sound like a dick or nothin,' but it says on your chart that you're fucked up. Ah, you talk like a fag, and your shit's all retarded. What I'd do, is just like ... ha ha ... like ... aha ... you know, like, you know what I mean, like ... ha ha ...

The film was a flop. Fox delayed its release and then sent it to a handful of theatres without any of the usual press and publicity fanfare. A number of articles about the movie's marketing troubles suggested that it was just too dark and harsh, that it risked insulting the audience. *Idiocracy* also took vulgar liberties with popular brand names, potential sponsors that the Fox combine did not wish to offend. However, like *Office Space,* Judge's 1999 workplace satire, *Idiocracy* has become something of a cult hit. It is especially popular on the

Internet. Many Net-dwellers defend it in their blogs and on movie sites such as imdb.com; they post comments like "*Idiocracy* is a documentary" and quotes from the movie in response to the latest Darwin Award–winning stunt, idiotic political gaffe, or outrageous comment from the likes of Glenn Beck. When Web wags mock Beck's blubbering with bits from *Idiocracy,* they are fighting Fox . . . with Fox.

Chapter Seven

IF YOU'RE SO SMART,
WHY AIN'T YOU RICH?

I used to act dumb. That act is no longer cute.

— PARIS HILTON[1]

nce when I was teaching a class, I made an offhand comment about Paris Hilton that was half joke, half example. I do not recall which fictional dimbulb I was comparing her to, but I vividly remember the young man who disagreed with me. Paris Hilton must be smart, he said. She had all that money and got all that attention, didn't she? I don't know if that young dude had ever heard the phrase "If you're so smart, why ain't you rich?" but that was his position.

He wasn't being argumentative. He was a solid student, and simply stating a fact. His comment revealed the gap between my definition of smarts and the way many of the students in that dude's class – a required intro to English full of career-minded majors – defined smarts. No wonder broke-ass scribblers such as Edgar Allan Poe did not interest or impress them much. If wealth is the ultimate measure of intelligence and money the surest proof of brains, then Paris trounces low-earning losers like poets and philosophers. Posthumous fame, book fame, nerd fame is not like the good kind of fame. It might last for centuries and let antique egg-heads torture the young from beyond the grave, but it just doesn't pay the bills.

It's hardly surprising that our culture cranks out students who think Paris Hilton is smart because she is successful, because she is rich. Many of them are in school so they can be rich and successful too. Rising college costs and increasing student debt loads have made education a big investment, which leads to increased pressure to pick a practical major that will pay out. Of course, this kind of calculation some-times backfires. When a glut of students rushes the same pro-fession, it is harder for them to get those guaranteed, sure-thing jobs, and the cushy incomes they were promised often drop. Job markets keep on shifting while the students spend the four to seven years it takes to get a bachelor's plus a master's or a professional credential or trade certification.

Hallmark should make a combination congraduations/ condolences card for those unfortunate students who finally finish only to discover that the world is already lousy with underemployed lawyers or IT professionals. Nevertheless, we routinely encourage eighteen-year-old North Americans to think about post-secondary education as if they were deciding what they are going to do for the rest of their lives. They aren't old enough to drink, but they are supposedly mature enough to pick the occupation that will eventually drive them to it.

If they choose wisely and work hard, they shall know comfort and ease and fine single malts for the rest of their days. If they pick the wrong major, attend the wrong school, or simply fuck up, they risk eternal loserdom, a life pock-marked with humiliations like cheap draft beer, renting, and public transit.

This hyperbolic, false choice presupposes that there are still such things as lifelong jobs, guaranteed majors, educational bets that always pay off. Most of us will end up trying several jobs, ones that may never add up to anything so lofty or lucrative as a career – or at least not the kind of career that college recruiters, guidance counsellors, and educrats sell to prospective students.

We tell students that education is important. But we also tell them that their educators are merely self-important, the inferior opening act for their bosses, who will determine their real worth in the real world. Here's one of my favourite examples of this kind of thinking. In Chapters Three and Four I mentioned the Spellings Commission, led by Bush's pal Margaret Spellings, who worked in his education departments when he was governor of Texas and president of the United States. In a 2006 college commencement address, which she delivered while she was secretary of education, Spellings told the following inspiring tale:

> I've always liked the story of the college student who got a C on his final paper because his idea was implausible. The idea [was] an overnight

delivery service. The student [was] Fred Smith. You may know him better as the CEO of FedEx.

So, don't let anyone else take the measure of your worth and capabilities. Always stand proud in who you are![2]

Once again we see the people who run companies, like the folks who win elections, triumph over the myopic old Poindexters who give their money-making insights C's.

Thanks, Secretary of Education, for totally undermining the concept of grades! It is also pretty rich and creamy to hear Spellings, who spent her entire tenure preaching the gospel of standardized tests, tell students they should never let anyone measure them. I thought her boss had said that measuring was the Gateway and education was the Key-Master, and defeating the Stay-Puft Marshmallow Man of low expectations was the civil rights issue of our time.

Spellings's story is a pithy summary of some common opinions: The only real ideas are lucrative ideas, business ideas. Popular success is the best evidence that an idea is plausible or worthwhile. Professorial types who criticize these ideas are just negative nellies. What do profs know about ideas? If they were really smart, they wouldn't be professors; they'd be running big companies like FedEx. So don't let their assessments of your capabilities get you down, kids. Let the C's slide off you like water off a duck's bum, for they matter not. The market is seated at the right hand of the Father and comes to judge all ideas, the living and the dead, the profitable and the wasteful, the useful and the useless.

It's ludicrous to assert that nerds run the world when they don't even run the bloody Department of Education. Again, this is not an exclusively American phenomenon. Ontario Premier Mike Harris demonstrated his commitment to common sense when he appointed a minister of education, John Snobelen, who had dropped out of school in grade 11. He had the necessary qualifications: he was a successful businessman, a credential that trumps any piece of paper from a college or school board. An H.P.D. (huge pile of dough) is always better than a Ph.D.

The commonsensical allege that nerds, especially useless humanities nerds, are Nosy Parkers, always sticking our schnozzes where they do not belong. We misuse our phony book-learnin' to pontificate about the real world, where our theoretical knowledge just does not apply. What a load of hooey!

This is factually and morally wrong. First, it is the money-minded, not the brainy, who currently occupy the bully pulpit. The moneyed are perpetually instructing us, telling us how we should run schools, universities, hospitals, and the government. They are proud of their particular expertise and they apply it to every institution and field of human endeavour. Bosses and business executives, and their hired brains in think tanks and lobbies, pitch solutions to public problems – or at least the same couple of solutions – over and over again. Biz groups such as the Chambers of Commerce and the Conference Board love schooling teachers and professors by telling us how to do our work. Apparently we should stop wasting so much goddamn money while simultaneously doing a much better job teaching their future employees how to read and write, do math, and understand science and technology.

Second, we nerds are citizens too. Pseudo-populists try to convince the public that the ivory tower is some distant imaginary realm and the language people learn there is some exotic foreign tongue. They continue to sell this line in spite of the growth of professional programs and the countless links between university and industry. Ostracizing nerds and undermining universities helps politicians and business leaders pre-empt any expert criticism. If some nerd releases a study that suggests a particular policy or product is a bad idea, it is very easy for politicians and CEOs to deflect and diminish it. It's a *study*, and everyone knows those things come from cloud-cuckoo-land.

Ordering nerds to butt out of public matters and confine their kooky readings to the classroom is an important part of the "shut up, quit whining, and get back to work" ethos of idiocracy. Idiocratic politicos may act as if economics is the only true expertise, the kind of thinking that matters most, but this is belied by their actions. They spend scads of spondulicks on the services of image consultants, speech writers, spokespeople, and communications experts.

The oft-maligned liberal arts teach people to analyze language, stories, and images, which are just as real and politically relevant as the latest numbers from the Dow-Jones or the Toronto Stock Exchange. Words and images are the marrow and sinews of personality politics, and the 2008 U.S. election demonstrated that personality is an increasingly important part of political life. The anti-rhetorical rhetoric of pols such as Harper, Palin, and McCain, with its endorsements of "common sense" and "action" and insulting references to "talk" and "ideas," is still rhetoric. It sure would be great if idiocrats could address their constituents while somehow avoiding the sissifying taint of words, but it's tough to give a speech without the damn things.

Barack Obama's eloquence has triggered a backlash against language, a hostility towards words. For example, in a September 2008 interview with Sean Hannity, Sarah Palin defended John McCain's assertion that "the fundamentals of the economy are strong." This statement was a major gaffe, but the stalwart Palin soldiered on, arguing that Barack Obama's criticisms of McCain were unfair. The problem? When Obama criticized McCain for saying the economy was strong, he was just quibbling about mere words. Maybe McCain had picked the wrong words, but everybody knew what he *really* meant, so it was wrong to pick on his verbiage.[3]

Two salient details: Palin repeatedly mispronounced *verbiage* as "verbage," getting one of the words for words wrong. Second, she was making an argument that I have heard from a few intrepid students and see all over the Internet. It's unfair to criticize someone for the *way* they say something or the words they use. *What* they're saying really matters. Content, regardless of spelling, grammar, or diction, matters more than form. And anyone who says otherwise is a grammar Nazi, trying to score picky points, or an elitist, trying to distract you with technicalities, so they can dodge the real argument.

Again we see that words are not really *real,* or at least not as really real as the opinions and beliefs that they are supposed to convey. But those opinions and beliefs are made of language too, and cannot exist apart from it. Even numbers, which many consider more trustworthy than words, are still a part of language. Form and content are not as separable as Sarah Palin (and some of my students) would like to believe. Words are not just little red wheelbarrows that schlep our beliefs and opinions around. Words shape the way we think and the world we live in, so it's silly to pretend they are incidental, just so much static interfering with our real meaning.

I can sculpt a birthday cake out of shit and insist that I obviously mean *cake,* that my real intent is to wish you a happy birthday, but my intentions and protestations cannot turn crap into a delicious dessert. People who dismiss and devalue words sanction sloppy language and serve up crap that looks like cake, which leads to sloppy thinking. People who deny the power of words while they are wielding that very power are usually trying to deny the responsibilities that come with it.

Anti-rhetorical posturing is disingenuous. Palin may cop a dismissive attitude towards the "verbage," but she hires ghost writers too. She and Lynn Vincent, her co-author, compiled a heap of words to produce Palin's autobio, *Going Rogue: An American Life;* it's over four hundred pages long. Palin's op eds and lengthy Facebook missives are much more polished and verbally sophisticated than the word salads she dished up throughout the campaign, which suggests that language just might be important after all.

I don't want to keep prattling on about Palin-speak in all its disjointed splendour. But I do want to single out one of her verbal tics, since I think it says something about the relationship between the way we speak and the way we think.

When Palin talks about her own accomplishments, she uses simple, active verbs: *I fixed, I cut, I kept progressing the state of Alaska,* and so forth. But when she needs to address serious political problems, she slides into the passive voice. There were a couple of good examples of this in her vice-presidential debate with Joe Biden. When she was talking about the meltdown on Wall Street, she said, "There have been so many changes in the conditions of our economy in just even these past weeks that there has been more and more revelation made aware now to Americans about the corruption and the greed on Wall Street." She also went passive when the moderator asked her about global warming. Palin agreed that it was real, but went on to say that there "is something to be said also for man's activities, but also for the cyclical temperature changes on our planet."[4]

There are situations when the passive voice is appropriate, but Palin's passive voice is weasel speak. The passive form, like the PR classic "Mistakes were made," posits a world where things get done to things. Nobody does anything, so nobody is responsible for anything. The explicit themes of Palin's speeches are rugged individuality and personal responsibility, but her language dissolves and dissipates that responsibility.

Right-wingers and real-worlders tend to see language as instrumental. Words are a set of power tools. They are ways to sell stuff and get people riled up to vote. Frank Luntz, a

Republican pollster and spinsmith, has made a fortune selling righties and major corporations the right verbal tools. Don't say *estate tax, domestic wiretapping,* or *public option;* use *death tax, electronic surveillance,* and *government option* instead.

When politicians use phrases like "straight talk" because consultants like Luntz tell them average folks love straight talk, they are not delivering straight talk. Quite the opposite – they're mouthing a buzzword. But if that buzzword gets the right emotional response, then it has done its job. Words are sharp sticks, poking and prodding till they stir up the hornets' nests that slumber in the heads of potential voters.

When right-wingers and real-worlders claim words do not matter, they are nerd-bashing, taking a few whacks at the wordy elite. But they are also saying that their instrumental understanding of language is the only valid one. Language, like reason, is only a tool, something people use to achieve other ends, such as wealth and power. Ergo, the majority of people who work with language, such as journalists, teachers, and professors, are mere hobbyists, people who do a lot of hammering but never manage to build a house.

Language is one of the main staging grounds for the culture wars that have raged since the 1980s. For example, the English Only movement has waxed and waned in accordance with the public's anxiety about illegal immigration and America's shifting racial demographics. When Clinton was in office, the economy was humming and unemployment was low, so the government was able to pass some legislation offering government services in funny foreign language. Now that the economy is in the toilet, the jobs are gone, and the president has a funny foreign name, the English Only movement is back.

"Speak English!" is definitely one of the planks in the Fox News/teabagger platform. Here's an example from one of the town hall meetings of 2009. On September 2, Representative Jim Hines was taking questions from his constituents in Norwalk, Connecticut. A bishop named Emilio Alvarez wondered if it would be okay if he asked his question in Spanish. Hines is fluent in Spanish, so he agreed, but his response was drowned out by the crowd. The auditorium erupted in loud, sustained boos and cries of "You're in the United States of America!" and "English! *English!*"

When Hines tried to translate the question for the yelping yahoos, he made a point of underlining that the bishop was a clergyman as he tried to placate, or maybe reproach, the crowd. A woman in the crowd responded, "He oughta speak English." The bishop might be doing the Lord's work, but that did not give him the right to sully her ears with that taco talk.[5]

In this instance, *English* is a polite way of saying *white* and *American.* "Speak English!" is rude, but it's still more acceptable than "Don't be so brown!" or "Go home!" This equation of *English* and *American* means that the people who love Sarah Palin for her sassy straight talk also cast themselves as English's true defenders. They are not racists or xenophobes but knights, crusaders protecting their virtuous mother tongue against scurrilous incursions by foreign invaders. Government forms *en español* are only the beginning. What other horrors does the shadow tyranny of King Juan Carlos portend?

This wing-nut allegiance to English clashes with the belief that words are not important – with comic results. Many English Only types are not very good at English. For example, there's a great photograph of an incensed middle-aged woman at a protest in Texas, her shirt festooned with flags, brandishing a sign that reads "Make English America's Offical Language." Many of the tea-party signs also boasted misspellings, whimsical use of quotation marks, and a festival of factual errors. My favourite was the one that read "Obama: More Czars than the USSR" – an awesome example of something that is so wrong it is right.

There are certainly Canadians who are anti-immigrant, and those who worry that immigrants are not assimilating, but there isn't the same hue and cry about English here. When Canadians bitch about official bilingualism, it does not really carry the same cultural and political charge as the complaints of the English Only movement. The majority of Canadians who object to official bilingualism hate it because it wastes money. It offends their parsimony, not their patriotism. People grumble about the Bloc Québécois squandering the rest of the country's time and money by thwarting the possibility of a majority Liberal or Conservative government.

Such complaints have little to do with language. English was certainly a political issue for Quebeckers circa Bill 101, but French is not really a political flashpoint in the rest of Canada the way Spanish is in the United States. The rhetoric does not come to the same rolling boil. When someone asks a question in French at a Canadian meeting, people wait for someone to repeat it in English, summon up their scraps of high-school

French, or zone out. Speaking another language is not a boo-worthy offence.

Hostility towards words, imported and domestic, is not confined to politics. It is also evident in consumer culture. Coffee ads are a good example. Since lattes have become shorthand for the nerd elite, advertisers must convince potential customers that they can enjoy delectable caffeinated beverages without all that obnoxious, snobby culture. The campaign for McDonald's line of McCafé drinks featured two similar ads, one with two girls and one with two boys. When the pairs discover that McDonald's finally has lattes, they are jubilant. The boys are thrilled that they can shave their goatees, take off their fake glasses, and watch football. The girls are delighted that they can stop listening to all that wretched jazz and pretending they know French; they can toss their books and read gossip mags again. No longer need these young people live a pretentious lie to avail themselves of premium coffee.

A similar, and similarly annoying, Dunkin' Donuts commercial begins with a chant of foreign coffee terms, a dirge of *mokkachokkolatte.* Then the people standing in line for coffee sing, "My mouth can't form these words . . . Is it French? Is it Italian? Perhaps Fritalian?" This is a shot at Starbucks' pseudo-Euroisms such as *venti,* which is about as foreign as *Häagen-Dazs.* But it is also saying "English only" in its own corporate way. Foreign words are onerous or pretentious, even though English itself is a hodgepodge of them.

Far'n-bashing is part and parcel of anti-intellectualism. Far'n-bashing usually involves Yerp, which usually means France. I won't revisit the bad old days of wine-dumping and freedom fries. But Mitt Romney is still in the running for the 2012 Republican slot, and he rocks the Francophobia like it's 2003. To be fair, Romney was anti-France before hating France was cool. When he was in college, he dodged the Vietnam draft by waging spiritual war in France, where he did his required Mormon prototyping.

For Romney, France is like a bizarro America – her godless, socialist, pathetic double. The *Boston Globe* managed to get its paws on a campaign document, a seventy-seven-page PowerPoint presentation, that outlined Romney's strategy. One page bore an equation: "Hillary = France," and another was emblazoned with a tricolour clip-art version of *le mauvais pays* and instructions to hit France hard. When Romney announced he was quitting the race in February 2008, he said, "I am convinced that unless America changes course, we will become the France of the 21st century – still a great nation, but no longer the leader of the world, no longer the superpower. And to me, that is unthinkable."[6] The Romney camp also had plans for a bumper sticker with the same theme: "First, Not France." Which is another way of saying money, not brains.

In an August 2007 speech, Romney maintained that he loves France, even speaks French himself. Heck, his kids were on vacation in France right then! France was just one of a list of bogeymen that Romney was planning to deploy in the campaign. He was also girding his loins for battle against

Hollywood, Hillary, and Massachusetts, the depraved socialist hellhole he governed from 2003 to 2007.

The Romney documents show that his team was concerned that the public thought he was a flip-flopper. Flip-flopping is a grievous charge. The valorization of certitude, the idea that staunch belief is a political virtue, means that anyone who changes his mind appears weak or vacillating.

It's absurd to call a politician a flip-flopper when he changes his mind because the situation changes or because he learns something new. That's not flip-flopping; it's sentience. But Romney is flip-flopping like a fish on a floor, trying to pick the most politically expedient positions, conjuring convenient devils to raise hackles and funds. What can anyone reasonably expect politicians to do about Hollywood? Is bringing back the Hays Production Code an urgent action item? Of course not. Romney's words are only means to ends, ways to win.

The creepy spectre of Euro-socialism has so inflamed the right that they now require classic Continental baddies such as Mussolini's Italy, Hitler's Germany, and Stalin's Russia to represent the bleak American future. But right-wingers continue to make disparaging remarks about the French. The health-care debate provided irresistible opportunities to dispute the claim that the French health-care system is the best in the world. How could it be? It's a government-run program, and they always fail.

Anti-French invective is another form of nerd-bashing, but it sure is funny hearing it from someone who is wearing a Ben Franklin costume. The right's heroes, the guys they name-check in their books and speeches, the guys they dress up as at rallies, all admired the French. They *relied on* the French. French ideas inspired the men who wrote America's founding documents, and French funds helped pay for their muskets and gunpowder. Without the help of the French, and the fancy French thought that real Americans sneer at, there wouldn't be an America at all. *Sacre vache,* y'all would be speaking British!

This part of America's history – the fact that the founders were nerds, not bullies – is conveniently omitted from the idiocratic version of the American Revolution, which is the story of a bunch of Joe Six-Packs getting mad as hell and deciding they weren't gonna take it anymore. They stood up! They fought! You do not often hear the right enthuse about the long hours the Founding Fathers spent thinking, reading philosophical texts, and crafting the documents that teabaggers wave at protests and pretend to defend. I guess "They sat down! They wrote!" just doesn't have the same zing.

The tea-partiers are a minority, and an extreme one at that, but their beliefs are paranoid, cartoon versions of opinions that the moderate majority hold too. You can't trust the government or big business, in that order. The only thing you can trust is the people. Freedom is the highest value: it decrees that I get to do what I like, spend my money how I please, and rear my progeny however I see fit.

These beliefs are totally mainstream. We see them in TV shows and movies. We hear them in pop music; rappers and redneck country singers agree that every North American is free to get rich. We see these beliefs in ads all the time.

Corporations play on public distrust, selling themselves as the only company that really cares about you, the lone honest broker or quality product in a world of lies and junk. Advertisers also love freedom-speak. Each innovation, no matter how minor, represents a liberation. McCafé ends the elitist stranglehold on espresso. Lysol leaves us germ-free. Vanilla toothpaste delivers us from the tyranny of mint.

As I argued in Chapter Five, freedom's most vocal defenders often end up trivializing it, defining it in merely selfish ways, such as the right to pick your favourite flavour or to teach your kid that global warming is a hoax. The right to be cheap, to hang on to one's hard-earned dough, is paramount. "Why should *I* have to pay for that?" is the standard idiocratic objection to public spending on the arts and social services.

I'm perfectly happy to pay taxes so kids and poets can eat, and I have no interest whatsoever in purchasing bombs or building hockey arenas. But Canada includes people who love hockey and people who love poetry and people who love both, people who want a bigger military and people who want to cut defence spending. So I am not always going to get what I want, and that's the price of being part of a *we*. That's a price that people seem increasingly unwilling to pay.

The idiocratic version of freedom undermines the public infrastructure that sustains freedom. The idiocratic bias against government is not a healthy skepticism; rather, it is destructive and nihilistic. Teabaggers and radical libertarians who dream of a world without taxes, without government, without public schools or hospitals are the logical conclusion of idiocracy's attempt to privatize all things public.

The desire to privatize is based on the myth of "the people." Politicians on both sides of the aisle are forever saying that "the people" are good; it is Ottawa and Washington that are bad. But the people choose their representative black-guards and dispatch them to their respective capital hells. The people vote for bad governments and patronize corrupt corporations. Separating the people and their institutions is a lot like trying to pry apart content and form, what we say and how we say it. This is what pseudo-populism tries to do when it insists that the people are always trustworthy but the governments they elect are not.

Such assertions, like Palin's passive verbs, dissolve responsibility. Saying that the people are better than their government encourages the people to ignore or disdain the government. This gives politicians permission to suck at their jobs and then blame the profession – politics in general – for their failures.

Pseudo-populist politicians tell voters that they are smart, but they treat them like they are stupid. *Hard-working people know best! Here's a tax credit. Go get yourself something nice and don't worry your pretty little head about the deficit.* They use all kinds of emotive buzzwords, ploys, and props such as France and Hollywood, green forests and blue sweaters, to play the public. They hire consultants to study the public, focus-grouping and testing every message, so they can tell the people precisely what they want to hear. In short words. Over and over again. The subjects of these studies must really crank the dials on their approval meters whenever politicians praise the superior intelligence of "the people."

Telling people what they want to hear is much easier than telling them what they need to know or what the government plans to do. And listening to happy bullshit is easier than following the news and puzzling through the issues. The leaders don't have to go through the fuss and bother of explaining their complicated plans, and we don't have to feign interest in the tedious details. It's efficient and convenient. It cuts down on the "verbage." Everybody wins!

But lately lots of people seem to be losing. They're losing their jobs, losing their houses, losing their health insurance coverage, losing their pensions, losing their investments. They feel they are losing interest in the machinations of their minority government or losing their post-electoral hope. Some believe they are losing their country, and some of those people seem to be losing their minds. So who is really winning? The answer is glaringly obvious: the people with the highest scores.

Pseudo-populism creates what it claims to despise. Politicians cede control to financial markets, which are elitist, and proudly so. They are complicated intellectual constructs that average, non-fiscal folks have a very hard time deciphering, that use math and language beyond our ken. Advice and counsel about the market is a huge market. Countless websites, books, seminars, and advisors offer explanations of how the market really works and how you can make it work for you.

On Wall Street, experts run things at a remove from the commoners. Arcane specialized intelligence triumphs over common sense and hard work, and diabolical geniuses use their wicked gifts to flummox the average Joe. In market parlance, "smart money" refers to the big traders, firms like Goldman Sachs, which employ hired brains, complex computer programs, and sophisticated formulas. "Dumb money" is your average investor, small-timers sinking their savings into some stocks, the kind of guys and gals whom politicians talk about when they talk about the economy. Dumb money usually loses. Smart money usually wins.

Let's look at those anti-nerd allegations I listed in the first chapter, and see how many of them accurately describe the moneyed brains who brought you the market meltdown.

1.   The money-minded think they are better than you.

In February 2008, CNBC reporter Rick Santelli, broadcasting from the floor of the Chicago Mercantile Exchange, went on a rant about government plans to assist people who could not pay their mortgages. He was outraged that the government was promoting bad behaviour. He suggested that it allow people to vote online, holding a referendum to see if folks really wanted to pay "the losers' mortgages." Santelli argued that the government should give money to those who know what to do with it, rewarding the "people that can carry the water, instead of drink the water."[7]

The traders cheered and applauded. They are the winners, the water-carriers, the ones who create value. The rest of us simply cannot be trusted with nice things like money or houses. This blame-the-victim explanation for the fiscal crisis was quite popular. It was the least knowledgeable participants who had crashed the system. The suckers and losers, the foreclosed folks at the bottom of the housing pyramid, were the bad guys. The experts who created and sold those mortgages, and then chopped them up and bundled them into complex investment instruments that supposedly made risks magically disappear, were not responsible.

But the losers who got mortgages they could not pay, who gambled on their houses and lost, were enthusiastically encouraged to do so by ostensible experts: mortgage brokers, the stock market, the government. Throughout the housing bubble, governments and markets told everyone that they were entitled to own a house or exploit the value of their home. The losers just drank the water that the traders, and their friends in the government, carried.

Who were the bigger losers? The family who lost their home or the swaggering geniuses who lost other people's billions, who raised and razed the value of North America's pension funds and stock portfolios?

The people who caused the crisis argued that they were the only ones expert enough to fix it. It was crucial to keep providing large salaries and bonuses, else the talent take their expertise elsewhere. Winners and water-carriers are entitled to lavish compensation because they are winners and water-carriers, regardless of how many losses they generate or how many wells they poison. Which brings us to . . .

2.   The money-minded expect money for nothing.

Matt Taibbi, a political reporter for *Rolling Stone*, has written a series of articles about the frauds that riddle Wall Street, describing the market as a "mountain of paste." He goes on to say: "Innovations like the ones that triggered the global collapse – credit-default swaps and collateralized debt obligations – were employed for the primary purpose of synthesizing out of thin air those revenue flows that our dying industrial economy was no longer pumping into the financial bloodstream."[8] Making and marketing decent products is sooo last century. Now money makes money from money. The money-minded made oodles of money placing bets on bets, selling and reselling money that was not really there or theirs, trading loans that consumers could not pay and banks could not cover.

We treat the stock market like a reliable indicator, something that shows us how the economy is really doing. But the economy of the finance sector has become increasingly estranged from the economy that most of us live in. Unemployment and foreclosure rates are still high and consumer confidence is still low, but so long as the Dow is above 10,000, all is right with the world. Hooray, bank profits are back up again too! Their big revenue generator? Overdraft fees.

The creation of wealth and the creation of value are two different things. Traders can generate vast paper fortunes that do not contribute anything to the economy, that do not get ploughed into the creation of new businesses or jobs. Bets on bets based on purely notional assets may make the smart money a quick buck, but they do not create work or good products or value. Instead, they simply Hoover up the dumb money and funnel it to the smart so they can gamble among themselves and generate more chimerical wealth by placing meta-bets on bets on ious.

3.   **The money-minded are social engineers who want to
     run the world.**

The money-minded are much more powerful than the average
nerd. It's hard to imagine any group of nerds causing such
widespread panic and urgent government action and costing
citizens so much. For example, the scientific community has
been warning us for years that Earth's ice is melting. We hem
and haw about that problem, and so do our governments.
But when it was money that started melting, it was a serious
crisis, prompting immediate, drastic measures. The imaginary money, the fortunes wrought of paste, are important
enough to require public protection and care. The planet?
Not so much.

     The great deregulation that commenced in the 1980s has
given money three freedoms that make it extraordinarily
powerful. Free marketeers are free from oversight and rules
concocted by petty bureaucrats. But they are also free to inter-
vene in public policy and free to draw on the public purse.
The money-minded have been insulting government for
nearly thirty years, but every time the moneyed lose vast
sums, they traipse to the capital for emergency capital. More
often than not, their bailout wishes are granted. And those
infusions of taxpayer dollars – yet another example of dumb
money slurped up by the smart – free the market to start creating its next crisis.

4.   **The money-minded live in a candy-coloured dream world.**
Remember the Internet boom and its prognostications,
such as Dow 36,000? When the Internet bubble popped, at

least we still had porn and Google. But Greenspan and company got America out of that bubble by creating another one – a worse one, which has bequeathed nothing but piles of bad paper and foreclosed subdivisions ruled by cougars and gators.

In 2005 David Lereah, chief economist for the National Association of Realtors, released the housing bubble version of Dow 36,000: a book with the girthy title *Are You Missing the Real Estate Boom? The Boom Will Not Bust and Why Home Prices and Other Real Estate Investments Will Climb Through the End of the Decade – and How to Profit from Them.* Lereah appeared frequently on CNBC and was beyond bullish. In January 2007 he said that things had finally hit bottom. He was shit-canned that same year.

In a *Wall Street Journal* interview, Lereah claimed that he was just following orders when he enthused about housing prices going up forever. The NAR pooh-poohs that, stating, "Realtors are the most trusted source for real estate information."[9] That's like calling crack dealers the most trusted source for crack-related inquires.

In my first book, *Your Call Is Important to Us,* which came out the same year as Mr. Lereah's, I said that there would be *beaucoup de* foreclosures when Greenspan's low, low interest rates rose. I'm not bragging. I know next to nothing about the real estate market and absolutely nothing compared to an expert like Mr. Lereah. But I knew that there would be a housing bust because I know that interest rates go up as well as down. And that house prices go down as well as up.

The people who said that this boom would never go bust did so for two reasons. Some were just being deceitful, hucksters churning up hype to sell more junky investments and tricksy mortgages. But others were delusional and they actually believed their own hype. The narrow technical proficiency that helped engender investment instruments like credit-default swaps and derivatives blinded marketeers. They lost sight of the big picture, the broader economic and social trends, which eventually rattled and wrecked everything they had built based on their complex theoretical models.

5.   The money-minded are hung up on the past.

Sadly, no. Would that this were so. The money-minded have the opposite problem. Trading happens faster than ever, thanks to new computer models that move capital in milliseconds. The moneyed, like the media, are always seeking the new new thing. They never learn from their own history. Instead they forget the crashes and collapses of the past, whether they are as recent as the dot-com bust or as old as tulipmania. Or they claim that the old rules of finance no longer apply, acting as if we now live in an alchemical economy that can transform bad debts into good assets and spin gold from clutching at straws. All those New Deal fiscal regulations that Clinton and Bush repealed were put in place to prevent speculative excesses and market instability. But the money-minded argued that the regulations were outdated, antique, nothing but a drag on the brave new economy with its new technologies and trading formulas.

One whistle-blower, Brooksley Born, a lawyer who briefly chaired the Commodity Futures Trading Commission, tried to warn the government that derivatives were exceedingly risky, but she was elbowed out of office by Greenspan and his posse. Born was flabbergasted by Greenspan's breezy attitude towards fraud. *Let the market sort it out,* the head of the Fed said. *It isn't the government's job to regulate that. The market is the best judge of the real and the fake.*[10] Look where that thinking got us.

6.   The money-minded are too negative.

If only. Again, the money-minded have the opposite problem. They are great fans of positive thinking, spending heaps of cash on motivational speakers and yes-you-can seminars. They are never negative about their own bailiwick, about the imaginary world of credit and investments. They reserve their negativity for the losers who are dumb enough to actually buy their spurious mortgages and investments. Or they wax negative about every other field of human endeavour.

It is preposterous that a group of people who enrich themselves by making meta-bets on bets on assets that do not exist get to serve as the arbiters of reality, the judges of the useful and the useless. How dare these paper-churners, whose trades take place in milliseconds, denigrate institutions that have lasted for more than a thousand years or texts that have endured for centuries?

Free marketeers claim that the market is the ultimate reality, the serious business of the world, precisely because it has become so unreal. Market fundamentalists need to impugn the reality of the liberal arts, of the sciences, so that their ideals, illusions, and delusions prevail. They hate any competing interpretation of the world, any ranking or hierarchy that is not monetary. This is why they detest government and do everything in their power to lobby and infiltrate it, to ensure that democratic values do not interfere with market values. This is also why they hate grades, and mock them constantly. How dare a nerd like me judge someone, based on my imaginary expertise? It's the market's job to figure out who is smart and who is stupid.

In February 2009 the *New York Times* ran an article called "In Tough Times, the Humanities Must Justify Their Worth." Whenever the economy tanks, as it did during the Reagan recession, enrolment in the liberal arts drops. And budget cuts at universities generally start with the so-called frills like reading, writing, and history. Hell, even the American Association of Universities and Colleges recommended scuttling the old ivory-tower view of education and emphasizing the practical (i.e., fiscal) benefits of a liberal arts degree.

This is an understandable reaction to the cost-cutting climate, but it is also capitulation to the ignorance and anti-intellectualism that currently prevail. Nerds had nothing to do with this crisis. They have nothing to apologize for or explain. Why should disciplines that have existed for thousands of years, books and ideas that humans have deemed valuable for centuries, have to justify their existence to the money-minded? And how can they, when they have such radically different values? The narrow, calculating, attention-deficit-disordered priorities of the moneyed make it impossible for the humanities to justify themselves without tossing their own values and joining the technically brilliant, ethically vacant idiots on Team Money.

If there were more liberal arts nerds, fewer business majors, and less social pressure to become a business major, then the 2008 market crisis might not have been so complex and sweeping. Another *Times* article, from March 2009, wondered, "Is It Time to Retrain B[usiness] Schools?" Note that the business schools, which got us into this mess, need not justify *their* existence. They offer a popular product, so they have every right to be. The article went on to say that M.B.A. programs were chock full of cheaters. M.B.A. students cheat more than students in any other discipline; one study showed that the majority, 56 per cent, cheated on their assignments. Why did they cheat? Because everyone else was cheating, so whatevs. Cheating was the only way to get ahead, and getting ahead is the only thing that matters.

The popular opinion that the economic world is the only real one, and that economic freedom is the only substantive freedom, is ignorant and destructive. Hannah Arendt calls this confusion of free enterprise and human freedom a "monstrous falsehood." She writes:

> Free enterprise, in other words, has been an unmixed blessing only in America, and it is a minor blessing, compared with the truly political freedoms, such as freedom of speech and thought,

of assembly and association, even under the best conditions. Economic growth may one day turn out to be a curse rather than a good, and under no conditions can it either lead into freedom or constitute a proof for its existence.[11]

The more-money-than-brains mindset confuses two things. It treats money as an end in itself and knowledge as a mere means to an end. When we treat money this way, we sanction the kind of excesses that crashed the stock markets and damaged the economy. We encourage students to mistake low cunning and greed for intellect and skill. When we treat knowledge as a mere means to an end, we create contraptions without regard for the consequences. A mob of yobs can burn your town down, but it takes brains – dangerous brains – to build technical triumphs such as nuclear bombs, electronic surveillance systems, derivatives, and the communications strategies that sell them to the public and the powers-that-be. When reason becomes instrumental, a tool, we also end up dismissing all kinds of knowledge that cannot be swiftly monetized for the benefit of the few.

Money is a means to various ends, a tool, and should be treated as such instead of serving as our ultimate good. Knowledge is a good, and when we give it the respect it deserves, it produces amazing things, including things with practical value. The market loves to hog the credit for inventions such as the computer, insisting that money did that, but this is just another way market fundamentalists advance their monopoly on the real. Most new inventions are the fruit of protracted nerdiness, of intellectual curiosity, that the market then popularizes and profits from.

The money-minded are building a future that has no use for the past or the public sector, one that tells kids they are free to choose to be engineers or entrepreneurs, a world made of bridges, banks, and barbarians. Philosophy, theology, history, and the sciences have all tried to crown themselves the Queen of Knowledge, the discipline that comprehends and transcends all the others. But economics and its younger brother, the business school, insist that the market is the Boss of Knowledge. Their fiscal daemons decide which knowledge is important and which is merely imaginary.

This is hubris. For the ancient Greeks, hubris was overweening pride and insolence, an arrogance that led people to tempt fate or flout the law and destroy themselves in the process. Free marketeers who believe that they know how things really work, who insult and dismiss other ways of understanding the world, mistake their technical savvy for total mastery. Any student of history or the great books knows that this is a serious mistake, the kind of careless thinking that courts disaster.

The humanities discourage hubris and counsel humility. The humanities teach us that those new new things that our friends in the market and the media chase are not very new at all. Stockbrokers and free marketeers are just alchemists with shinier, more expensive tools, money magicians trying to find the stock market version of the Philosopher's Stone that turns lead into gold.

The humanities are the best vaccine against intellectual infections such as hubris, dogmatism, and demagoguery. The humanities teach us to think in the long term, to consider the consequences of our actions instead of acting in the interest of expediency and convenience. The humanities teach us to be skeptical, to be critical and deliberative instead of reacting emotively, which leads us into frightened condemnation and frenzied cheerleading. Studying the humanities is a corrective insofar as it pulls us out of our presentism and forces us to confront something other than the narrow and the now.

The more-money-than-brains mindset tells us we should aspire to be useful. But who wants to be used? I'd rather be useless than used. Hardly any of the things that people use – their buildings and their bowls – survive the civilizations that create them. Our ancestors' most enduring and valuable legacy lives in their books, their ideas, their art, their music. Stains on paper, puffs of sonorous air, and unruly brainchildren may not seem as real as your bank balance or the latest GDP figures, but they are.

When we claim that the humanities are insignificant, imaginary, or obsolete, the fiscal alchemists win. But their triumphs are short-lived. Wealth, like life, is brief. The liberal arts are long. A humanities education has incalculable value, because its worth is beyond calculation, not beneath it. The humanities are despised because they are dangerous. They arm us with the intellectual weapons we need to fight the forces of ignorance and idiocracy, and to free ourselves from freedumb.

NOTES

<CHAPTER ONE: DON'T NEED NO EDJUMACATION>

CHAPTER ONE: DON'T NEED NO EDJUMACATION

1. Carlin Romano, "Obama, Philosopher in Chief," *Chronicle of Higher Education,* June 16, 2009. Available online at http://beta.chronicle.com/article/Obama-Philosopher-in-Chief/44524/.

2. See http://ignatieff.me/?p=ignatieff#economy.

3. Richard Hofstader, *Anti-intellectualism in American Life* (New York: Knopf, 1963).

4. *Real Time with Bill Maher,* HBO, June 19, 2009.

5. Perino made the admission on the NPR quiz show *Wait, Wait, Don't Tell Me* on December 8, 2007.

6. See http://www.thesecret.tv/behind-the-secret.html.

7. The op ed ran in the *New York Times* on September 24, 2008, p. A27. A longer version is available on her blog at http://ehrenreich.blogs.com/barbaras_blog/2008/09/how-positive-thinking-wrecked-the-economy.html. An even longer version of this argument is available in her most recent book, *Bright-Sided: How the Relentless Promotion of Positive Thinking Has Undermined America* (New York: Metropolitan Books, 2009).

8. *The Situation Room with Wolf Blitzer,* CNN, September 17, 2008.

CHAPTER TWO: AT THE ARSE END OF THE LATE, GREAT ENLIGHTENMENT

1. Immanuel Kant, "What Is Enlightenment?" in *Philosophical Writings*, ed. Ernst Behler (London: Continuum Press, 1993).

2. Glenn Beck, *Glenn Beck's Common Sense: The Case Against an Out of Control Government, Inspired by Thomas Paine* (New York: Threshold Press, 2009).

3. Debora Mackenzie, "End of the Enlightenment," *New Scientist*, October 8, 2005, p. 39.

4. George Monbiot, "The End of the Enlightenment," *The Guardian*, December 18, 2001. Available on his blog at http://www.monbiot.com/archives/2001/12/18/the-end-of-the-enlightenment/. Garry Wills, "The Day the Enlightenment Went Out," *New York Times*, November 4, 2004, p. A25. Available online at http://query.nytimes.com/gst/fullpage.htm l?res=9C0CE2DA173CF937A35752C1A9629C8B63.

5. Victor Davis Hanson, "Losing the Enlightenment," *Wall Street Journal*, November 29, 2006. Available online at http://www.opinionjournal.com/federation/feature/?id=110009312.

6. Theodor Adorno and Max Horkheimer, *Dialectic of Enlightenment*, ed. G. S. Noerr, trans. E. Jephcott (Stanford, CA: Stanford University Press, 2002).

7. Thomas Paine, *The Age of Reason*, ed. Moncure Daniel Conway (Mineola, NY: Dover Books, 2004).

8. Southern Baptist Convention, "Baptist Faith and Message," adopted at the 2000 convention and available online at http://www.sbc.net/BFM/bfm2000.asp.

9. See http://www.creationmuseum.org/about.

10. "Alberta Passes Law Allowing Parents to Pull Students Out of Class," CBC, June 2, 2009. Available online at

http://www.cbc.ca/canada/story/2009/06/02/alberta-human-rights-school-gay-education-law.html.

11. Quoted by Associated Free Press reporting from Dover, Pennsylvania, March 27, 2005.

12. John Locke, "The Second Treatise of Civil Government," in *The Portable Enlightenment Reader,* ed. Isaac Kramnick (New York: Penguin, 1995).

13. Thomas Paine, "Common Sense," ibid.

14. Voltaire, "On Commerce" (Letter Ten), in *Letters on England,* trans. Leonard Tancock (New York: Penguin Books, 2005).

15. Voltaire,"On the Presbyterians" (Letter Six), ibid.

16. David Hume, "Of Refinement in the Arts," in *Selected Writings,* ed. Stephen Copley and Andrew Edgar (New York: Oxford University Press, 1998).

17. Immanuel Kant, "On the Common Saying: This may be true in theory but it does not apply in practice," in *Political Writings,* ed. H. S. Reiss (New York: Cambridge University Press, 2003).

18. Jerry W. Knudson, *Jefferson and the Press: Crucible of Liberty* (Columbia: University of South Carolina Press, 2006).

19. Denis Diderot, *The Encyclopedia: Selections,* ed. Stephen J. Gendizer (New York: Harper and Row, 1967).

20. Patton Oswalt, *Werewolves and Lollipops* (SubPop Records, 2007).

21. Thomas Jefferson, Letter to George Wythe, August 16, 1789, in *The Political Writings of Thomas Jefferson,* ed. Merrill D. Peterson (Chapel Hill: University of North Carolina Press, 1993).

22. Bernard Weinraub, "Bush and Governors Set Education Goals," *New York Times,* September 29, 1989, p. A10.

CHAPTER THREE: IS OUR SCHOOLS SUCKING?

1. John Adams, "A Dissertation on Canon and Feudal Law," in *The Portable John Adams*, ed. John Patrick Diggins (New York: Penguin Books, 2004).

2. Lowell M. Rose and Alec Gallup, "39th Annual Phi Delta Kappa/Gallup Poll of the Public's Attitudes Towards Public Schools," in *Phi Delta Kappan*, September 2007, p. 33.

3. Canadian Education Association, *Public Education in Canada: Facts, Trends and Attitudes 2007*. Available online at www.cea-ace.ca.

4. The CBC survey results are available at http://www.cbc.ca/news/passorfail/.

5. The Center for Educational Reform tracks charter school numbers at http://www.edreform.com/Fast_Facts/K12_Facts/.

6. Results of Stanford's study on charter schools are available online at http://credo.stanford.edu/.

7. John Fitzgerald for Minnesota 2020, "Checking in on Charter Schools: An Examination of Charter School Finances." Available online at http://www.mn2020.org/index.asp.

8. Alvin P. Sanoff, "What Professors and Teachers Think: A Perception Gap over Students' Preparation," *Chronicle of Higher Education*, March 10, 2006, p. B9.

9. See http://www.fairtest.org/testing-explosion-0.

10. Dan Lips and Evan Feinberg, "The Administrative Costs of No Child Left Behind," Heritage Foundation, April 7, 2007. Available online at http://www.heritage.org/Press/Commentary/ed040907b.cfm.

11. Kevin Carey, "The Pangloss Index: How States Game the No Child Left Behind Act," Education Sector, November 13, 2007.

Available online at http://www.educationsector.org/research/
research_show.htm?doc_id=582446.

12. Claudia Wallis, "No Child Left Behind: Doomed to Fail?"
    Time, June 8, 2008. Available online at http://www.time.com/
    time/nation/article/0,8599,1812758,00.html.

13. "President Bush Discusses No Child Left Behind,
    Woodbridge Elementary and Middle School, Washington,
    D.C., October 5, 2006." Transcript available online at
    http://www.whitehouse.gov/news/releases/2006/10/
    20061005-6.html.

14. Will Woodward, "Teachers' Union Threatens Boycott of SATS,"
    The Guardian, April 2, 2002. Available online at http://www.
    guardian.co.uk/uk/2002/apr/01/politics.schools.

15. PISA data for 2000, 2003, and 2006 are available
    online at http://www.pisa.oecd.org/pages/0,2987,
    en_32252351_32235731_1_1_1_1_1,00.html.

16. The National Center for Education Statistics analysis of the
    PIRLS for 2001 and 2006 is available at their website, http://
    nces.ed.gov/pubsearch/pubsinfo.asp?pubid=2008017. For
    more information on the PIRLS, see its website at
    http://timss.bc.edu/.

17. James J. Heckman and Paul A. Lafontaine, "The Declining
    American High School Graduation Rate: Evidence,
    Sources, and Consequences," National Bureau of Economic
    Research. Available online at http://www.nber.org/
    reporter/2008number1/heckman.html.

18. Mitchell Landsberg and Howard Blume, "1 in 4 California
    High School Students Drop Out, State Says," *Los Angeles
    Times,* July 17, 2008, p. A2.

19. Young's essay is available online at http://www.guardian.
    co.uk/politics/2001/jun/29/comment.

20. You can access the latest stats on economic mobility at www.
    economicmobility.org, which is a collaborative research pro-
    ject involving the Pew Charitable Trusts and some opposing
    think tanks – the American Enterprise Institute, the Brookings
    Institution, the Heritage Foundation, and the Urban Institute.

21. One chart, for the GRE, is available at http://www.ncsu.
    edu/chass/philo/GRE%20Scores%20by%20Intended%20
    Graduate%20Major.htm. Philosophy departments have many
    of these charts, since philosophy majors usually score well on
    exit tests. There's another one at http://philosophy.acadiau.
    ca /why_phil/scores.htm, drawn from Clifford Adelman's
    study of standardized test scores of college students from
    the 1960s to the '80s. For more recent numbers, see Michael
    Nieswiadomy, "LSAT Scores of Economics Majors: The
    2003–2004 Class Update," available at http://economics.gcsu.
    edu/students/lsat.pdf.

22. You can still find *A Nation at Risk* online at http://www.
    ed.gov/pubs/NatAtRisk/index.html.

23. Greg Toppo, "'Nation at Risk': The Best Thing or the Worst
    Thing for Education?" *USA Today,* May 22, 2008. Available
    online at http://www.usatoday.com/news/education/2008-04-
    22-nation-at-risk_N.htm.

24. For more of her criticisms of textbooks, see Ravitch's *The
    Language Police: How Pressure Groups Restrict What Students
    Learn* (New York: Vintage Books, 2004). She has also written
    a history of U.S. school reforms that looks at the oscillation
    between vocational, progressive, and traditional notions of

education, *Left Back: A Century of Battles over School Reform* (New York: Simon and Schuster, 2001).

25. For more on the Texas textbook controversy, see "History's First Draft: Newt Gingrich But No Liberals," *Houston Chronicle*, August 20, 2009. Available online at http://www. chron.com/disp/story.mpl/metropolitan/6581189.html. Also, "State Education Board Shouldn't Rewrite History," *Dallas Morning News*, July 18, 2009. Available online at http://www. dallasnews.com/sharedcontent/dws/news/localnews/stories/ DN-olivera_18met.ART.State.Edition1.4bb2401.html.

26. Michael F. Shaughnessy, "An Interview with Diane Ravitch," EducationNews.org, March 2008. Available online at http:// ednews.org/articles/24020/1/An-Interview-with-Diane-Ravitch-On-Some-Current-Events/Page1.html.

CHAPTER FOUR: SCREW U OR HATE MY PROFESSORS

1. U.S. Department of Education, *Digest of Education Statistics,* 2008.

2. Association of Universities and Colleges of Canada, *Trends in Higher Education: Volume One – Enrolment,* 2007.

3. College Board, *Trends in College Pricing 2007.*

4. Figure from Statistics Canada's *Survey of Tuition and Living Accommodation Costs for Full-time Students at Canadian Degree-Granting Institutions,* October 18, 2007.

5. National Leadership Council for Liberal Education and America's Promise, *College Learning in the New Global Century,* January 10, 2007.

6. Jill Casner-Lotto and Linda Barrington, *Are They Really Ready to Work?,* released by the Conference Board in October 2006.

7.   Ibid.

8.   Spellings Commission, *A Test of Leadership: Charting the Future of U.S. Higher Education,* September 2006.

9.   American College Testing Program, *National Collegiate Retention and Persistence to Degree Rates, Trends 1983–2008.* More stats are available at the ACT educational website, www.act.org.

10.   Danielle Shaienks and Tomasz Gluszynski, *Participation in Postsecondary Education: Graduates, Continuers and Drop-outs: Results from YITS Cycle 4,* Statistics Canada, November 2007.

11.   Barbara Kay, "Liberate the Campus," *National Post,* October 24, 2007. Available online at http://network.nationalpost. com/np/blogs/fullcomment/archive/2007/10/24/barbara-kay-liberate-the-campus.aspx.

12.   Matthew Woessner and April Kelly-Woessner, "Left Pipeline: Why Conservatives Don't Get Doctorates," paper presented at the American Enterprise Institute conference "Reforming the Politically Correct University," November 2007.

13.   The press release announcing the Argus Project is available on-line at http://www.nas.org/polPressReleases.cfm?Doc_Id=278.

14.   David Horowitz, *The Professors: The 101 Most Dangerous Academics in America* (Washington, DC: Regnery Publishing, 2006).

15.   Russell Jacoby, "Gone and Being Forgotten," *Chronicle of Higher Education,* July 25, 2008, p. B5.

16.   Spellings Commission, *A Test of Leadership.*

17.   "Why Universities Should be Graded, Too," *Maclean's,* September 4, 2006. Available online at http://www.macleans. ca/article.jsp?content=20060904_132707_132707&source=srch.

18. Alan Finder, "Decline of the Tenure Track Raises Concerns," *New York Times,* November 20, 2007, p. A16.

19. Lindsay Waters, "Bonfire of the Humanities," *Village Voice,* August 24, 2004, p. 46.

CHAPTER FIVE: BULLY VS. NERD

1. H. L. Mencken, *A Book of Burlesques* (1916, reprinted by BiblioBazaar, 2007).

2. Chuck Todd, First Read blog, July 23, 2009. Available online at http://firstread.msnbc.msn.com.

3. Michael Hirsh, "Brains Are Back," *Newsweek,* November 7, 2008. Available online at http://www.newsweek.com/id/168032.

4. From a town hall meeting in Sun City, Arizona, August 25, 2009.

5. Greer issued his press release on September 1, 2009. The full text is available online at http://www.rpof.org/article. php?id=754.

6. Actor Craig T. Nelson, appearing on Glenn Beck's show, Fox News, May 28, 2009.

7. This gem was uttered by a protestor at a town hall meeting in Simpsonville, South Carolina, with Representative Robert Inglis and quoted by Phillip Rucker in "S.C. Senator Is a Voice of Reform Opposition," *Washington Post,* July 28, 2009.

8. Karl Marx, *The Communist Manifesto* (New York: International Publishers, 2001).

9. Robert Barnes, "Straight Talk Express's Limited Engagement," posted on The Trail, the *Washington Post*'s online campaign diary, August 14, 2008. Available online at http://voices. washingtonpost.com/44/2008/08/straight-talk-expresss-limited.html.

10. Richard Hofstader, *Anti-intellectualism in American Life* (New York: Knopf, 1963).

11. "Agnew Unleashed," *Time,* October 31, 1969. Available online at http://www.time.com/time/magazine/article/0,9171,839090-1,00.html.

12. Kenneth J. Hughes, Jr., "Nixon vs. the Imaginary 'Jewish Cabal,'" History News Network, September 24, 2007. Available online at http://hnn.us/articles/42970.html.

13. See Lou Cannon, *President Reagan: The Role of a Lifetime* (Jackson, TN: Public Affairs, 2000).

14. Reagan's 1985 address to the CPAC, "Creators of the Future," is available on the organization's website at http://www.conservative.org/pressroom/reagan/reagan1985.asp.

15. Evan Thomas, "The Left Starts to Rethink Reagan," *Newsweek,* May 3, 2008, p. 38.

16. See "The Mendacity Index," *Washington Monthly,* May 2003. Available online at http://www.washingtonmonthly.com/features/2003/0309.mendacity index.html.

17. See Jonathan Chait, *The Big Con: The True Story of How Washington Got Hoodwinked and Hijacked by Crackpot Economics* (New York: Houghton Mifflin, 2007).

18. George W. Bush, commencement address, Yale University, May 21, 2001.

19. George W. Bush, press conference, September 10, 2007. Transcript available at http://www.whitehouse.gov/news/releases/2007/09/20070920-2.html.

20. "Live Desk with Martha McCallum," Fox News, June 9, 2008. Transcript available online at Media Matters.org, http://mediamatters.org/items/200806100003.

21. See the transcript for Limbaugh's August 29, 2008, broad-cast online at http://www.rushlimbaugh.com/home/daily/site_082908/content/01125111.guest.html.

22. Tom Kizzia, "'Fresh Face' Launched, Carries Palin's Career," *Anchorage Daily News,* October 23, 2006. The paper posted this and other old Palin stories online during the 2008 campaign. Available at http://www.adn.com/sarah-palin/background/story/510447.html.

23. Chris Clizza, "McCain Manager: This Election Is Not about Issues," posted on The Fix, a *Washington Post* political blog, September 2, 2008. Available online at http://voices.washingtonpost.com/thefix/eye-on-2008/mccain-manager-this-election-i.html.

24. Jeffrey Lord, "Batman and Rush: Why McCain Will Win," *American Spectator,* August 19, 2008. Available online at http://www.spectator.org/dsp_article.asp?art_id=13726.

25. Jonathan Dignan, "(Less) Male, (Even Less) Educated, (Even Less) Experienced & (Even More) White," released by the Public Policy Forum in May 2009. Available online at http://www.ppforum.ca/publications/lessmale-even-less-educated-even-less-experienced-%0Beven-more-white.

26. See Calvin Trillin's "Paper Baron," a profile of Lord Black, on p. 62 of the December 17, 2001, issue of the *New Yorker* for more on Canada's "tall poppy" syndrome.

27. See Joe Klein, *Politics Lost: How American Democracy Was Trivialized by People Who Think You're Stupid* (New York: Doubleday, 2006).

28. The Rasmussen poll is available online at http://www.rasmussenreports.com/public_content/politics/

general_politics/february_2009/59_still_believe_government_is_
the_problem. The Gallup version is also online, at http://www.
gallup.com/poll/123101/Americans-Likely-Say-Government-
Doing-Too-Much.aspx.

CHAPTER SIX: MORE IS LESS

1. From *The State of the News Media, 2006,* the Project for
Excellence in Journalism's annual report.

2. "The Death of Journalism" appeared on Huckabee's
self-titled Fox News show on September 14, 2009. The
full text is available online at http://www.foxnews.com/
story/0,2933,550160,00.html.

3. Bill Bishop, "America's Partisan Reading List," The Big Sort
blog, Slate.com, posted October 29, 2008. Available online at
http://www.slate.com/blogs/blogs/bigsort/archive/2008/10/29/
the-many-ways-we-sort-ourselves.aspx.

4. Sacred Heart University's annual poll, "Trust and Satisfaction
with the Media," was released September 2009. Results are
available online at http://www.sacredheart.edu/pages/30046_
shu_national_poll_trust_and_satisfaction_with_the_
national_news_media.cfm.

5. Allison Hope Weiner, "The Web Site Celebrities Fear," *New
York Times,* June 25, 2007, p. C1.

6. Upton appeared on NBC's *Today* show on August 28, 2007.

7. Pew Research Center for People and the Press, "Press
Accuracy Rating Hits Two-Decade Low: Public Evaluations
of the News Media, 1985–2009," September 14, 2009. Full
results are available online at http://people-press.org/
report/543/#prc-jump.

8. Kris Kodrich, "Uncovering the Truth," *Denver Post*, October 22, 2009. Available online at http://www.denverpost.com/opinion/ci_13612051.

9. Anne Trubek, "We Are All Writers Now," More Intelligent Life blog, *The Economist*. Available online at http://www.moreintelligentlife.com/content/anne-trubek/we-are-all-writers-now.

10. "Clive Thompson on the New Literacy," *Wired*, August 24, 2009. Available online at http://www.wired.com/techbiz/people/magazine/17-09/st_thompson.

11. The full lists are available online at http://www.randomhouse.com/modernlibrary/100bestnovels.html.

12. John Markoff, "The Passion of Steve Jobs," BITS blog, *New York Times*, January 15, 2008.

13. National Endowment for the Arts, "Reading on the Rise," January 2009. The full report is available online at http://www.arts.gov/research/readingonRise.pdf.

14. The poll found that more Americans (73%) than Canadians (69%) read a book in the past year. See "Canadian Book Readers Fall Behind U.S.: Poll," Canwest News Service, January 1, 2008. Available online at http://www.canada.com/topics/news/national/story.html?id=81b3a991-6004-4ca8-8259-4d605e1cf767&k=50303.

15. Turner-Riggs for Department of Canadian Heritage, "The Book Retail Sector in Canada," September 2007. The full report is available online at http://www.pch.gc.ca/pgm/padie-bpidp/rep/rapp-rep_07/rapport-pdf-report-eng.pdf.

16. Craig Wilson, "Professor Pausch's Life, 'Lecture' Go from Web to

Book," *USA Today*, April 8, 2008. Available online at http://www.usatoday.com/life/books/news/2008-04-07-pausch_N.htm.

17. These figures are from the trade analysts Bowker's Books in Print database.

18. Liguori made the remark at the 2008 "upfronts," the presentation of the network's new shows. Available online at http://www.slate.com/id/2191209/.

19. Enjoy the clip yourself at http://www.youtube.com/watch?v=ANTDkfkoBaI&feature=related.

CHAPTER SEVEN: IF YOU'RE SO SMART, WHY AIN'T YOU RICH?

1. Paris said this to Barbara Walters, whom she had called collect from jail. It ran on ABC and was widely and swiftly quoted in both the old and new media.

2. Margaret Spellings, commencement address, Montgomery College (Montgomery County, MD), May 17, 2006.

3. The transcript of the Palin/Hannity interview is available on the Fox News website at http://www.foxnews.com/story/0,2933,424346,00.html.

4. The transcript of the vice-presidential debate is available on CNN's website at http://www.cnn.com/2008/POLITICS/10/02/debate.transcript/.

5. The clip was posted by a kindly soul named Connecticut Bob. You can watch the shit-show on YouTube at http://www.youtube.com/watch?v=VAEIcsOL2n4.

6. The *Wall Street Journal*'s Washington Wire has the full text of his speech at http://blogs.wsj.com/washwire/2008/02/07/text-of-romneys-speech-i-hate-to-lose/.

7. Santelli's rant is available on YouTube at http://www.youtube.com/watch?v=bEZB4taSEoA.

8. Matt Taibbi, "Wall Street's Naked Swindle," *Rolling Stone.* The online version, posted on October 14, 2009, is available at http://www.rollingstone.com/politics/story/30481512/wall_streets_naked_swindle/1.

9. Nancy Keates, "Realtors' Former Top Economist Says Don't Blame the Messenger," *Wall Street Journal,* January 12, 2009, p. A1.

10. An excellent episode of PBS's *Frontline* profiles Brooksley Born and her concerns about the financial system. It is called "The Warning," and you can watch it online at http://www.pbs.org/wgbh/pages/frontline/warning/?utm_campaign=homepage&utm_medium=proglist&utm_source=proglist.

11. Hannah Arendt, *On Revolution* (London: Penguin Books, 1963).